THE MORALLY DIVIDED BODY

The Pro Ecclesia Series

Books in The Pro Ecclesia Series are "for the Church." The series is sponsored by the Center for Catholic and Evangelical Theology, founded by
Carl Braaten and Robert Jenson in 1991. The series seeks to nourish the
Church's faithfulness to the gospel of Jesus Christ through a theology that
is self-critically committed to the biblical, dogmatic, liturgical, and ethical traditions that form the foundation for a fruitful ecumenical theology.
The series reflects a commitment to the classical tradition of the Church as
providing the resources critically needed by the various churches as they
face modern and post-modern challenges. The series will include books by
individuals as well as collections of essays by individuals and groups. The
Editorial Board will be drawn from various Christian traditions.

FORTHCOMING TITLES INCLUDE:

Christian Theology and Islam, edited by Michael Root and James J. Buckley

Who Do You Say That I Am?: Proclaiming and Following Jesus Today, edited
by Michael Root and James J. Buckley

The Morally Divided Body

Ethical Disagreement
and the Disunity of the Church

edited by

Michael Root &
James J. Buckley

 CASCADE *Books* · Eugene, Oregon

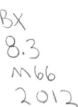

THE MORALLY DIVIDED BODY
Ethical Disagreement and the Disunity of the Church

The Pro Ecclesia Series 1

Cascade Books
An Imprint of Wipf and Stock Publishers
199 W. 8th Ave., Suite 3
Eugene, OR 97401

www.wipfandstock.com

ISBN 13: 978-1-61097-764-7

Cataloging-in-Publication data:

The morally divided body : ethical disagreement and the disunity of the church / edited by Michael Root and James J. Buckley.

x + 146 p. ; 23 cm. —Includes bibliographical references.

The Pro Ecclesia Series 1

ISBN 13: 978-1-61097-764-7

1. Church—Unity. 2. Ecumenical movement. 3. I. Root, Michael, 1951–. II. Buckley, James J. III. Title. IV. Series.

BX8.3 .M66 2012

Manufactured in the U.S.A.

Contents

Contributors

Frederick Christian Bauerschmidt is Associate Professor of Theology and Chair of the Department of Theology at Loyola University Maryland as well as a deacon of the archdiocese of Baltimore. He is the author of *Julian of Norwich and the Mystical Body Politic of Christ* (1999), *Why the Mystics Matter Now* (2003), *Holy Teaching: Introducing the Summa Theologiae of St. Thomas Aquinas* (2005), and numerous articles.

James J. Buckley is Professor of Theology at Loyola University Maryland. He is a member of the American-Lutheran Catholic dialogue and associate director of the Center for Catholic and Evangelical Theology. He contributed to and edited *The Blackwell Companion to Catholicism* (2008).

Robert W. Jenson has taught theology and philosophy at liberal arts colleges, universities and a theological seminary. His last full-time appointment was as Senior Scholar for Research at the Center of Theological Inquiry in Princeton. His most recent book is *Canon and Creed* (2010).

Michael Root is Professor of Systematic Theology at The Catholic University of America and Executive Director of the Center for Catholic and Evangelical Theology. He was formerly the Director of the Institute for Ecumenical Research, Strasbourg, France.

Beth Barton Schweiger teaches early American history at the University of Arkansas. She is the author of *The Gospel Working Up: Progress and the Pulpit in Nineteenth-Century Virginia* (2000), coeditor of *Religion in the American South* (2004), and author of "Seeing Things: Knowledge and Love in History," in *Confessing History: Explorations in Christian Faith and the Historian's Vocation* (2010).

Joseph D. Small served for twenty-three years as Director of the Office of Theology and Worship, Presbyterian Church (USA). He is the author of *To Be Reformed: Living the Tradition* (2010), and has edited and contributed to *Let Us Reason Together: Christians and Jews in Conversation* (2010), *Proclaiming the Great Ends of the Church* (2010), and *Conversations with the Confessions: Dialogue in the Reformed Tradition* (2005).

Susan K. Wood is Professor of Theology at Marquette University. She has published *Spiritual Exegesis and the Church in the Theology of Henri de Lubac* (1998), *Sacramental Orders* (2000; also translated into Spanish), and *One Baptism: Ecumenical Dimensions of the Doctrine of Baptism* (2009). She is the editor of *Ordering the Baptismal Priesthood* (2003) and coeditor with Alberto Garcia of *Critical Issues in Ecclesiology* (2011).

David Yeago is the Michael Peeler Professor of Systematic Theology at Lutheran Theological Southern Seminary, Columbia, SC. His textbook in systematic theology is forthcoming from Eerdmans.

Introduction

Michael Root and James J. Buckley

WHILE DOCTRINAL ISSUES HAVE often in the past been the most ecumenically neuralgic topics, increasingly today ethical issues—abortion and homosexuality most prominently—have become a focus of difference between the churches and of potentially splintering debate within churches. These issues are more laden with emotion than many traditional doctrinal disputes, but ecumenical discussions have yet to address them in detail. We have little sense of just when and how ethical disputes rightly impact communion within and among the churches. When can we live together with difference over such matters, and when does unity in Christ require common teaching?

In June 2010, the Center for Catholic and Evangelical Theology addressed these issues by devoting its annual conference to "The Morally Divided Body: Ethical Disagreement and the Disunity of the Churches." This collection of essays are the papers given at that conference.

It is important that these essays are only a beginning. We know we live in a Church and churches whose unity has been shattered by ethical disagreements, from the disagreements over rich and poor at Corinthian Eucharists to the ways slavery divided early American churches. These were very specific disputes. But, beyond such specific disputes, there are those tempted to believe and act as if such divisions do not matter as much as our supposed deeper unity—or as if such moral or ethical disagreements are the "real" disagreements, eclipsing any agreements on Scripture and creeds, justification by faith or the communion of saints. These essays cover this range of issues, from general ethical issues of why God cares about the way we live and how we know when ethical disagreements should divide the churches, to specific cases like nineteenth-century disputes about slavery and challenges to formulating Evangelical-Catholic consensus on ethical and moral matters. We are sure that more can and must be said about both the general and the specific issues. We aim at a beginning. We hope that the essays provide pastors and other Christians, including theologians interested in pastorally engaged theology, with resources for building or rebuilding the divided body.

1

Can Ethical Disagreement
Divide the Church?

Robert W. Jenson

THE FOLLOWING ESSAY IS—WHATEVER its errors or other faults—at least timely. For the question stated by its title is beyond much doubt the next great ecumenical stumbling block—or just possibly, and only by uncovenanted mercies of God, opportunity. Churches are dividing in themselves and from their ecumenical partners over matters that once were not even on the agenda. Many believers are desperate for their churches. Thus the 2010 conference of the Center for Catholic and Evangelical Theology, where an oral version of this essay was presented, drew the largest and most engaged crowd in the center's recent history.

To go with the question's actuality, there is its difficulty. An adequate treatment would deal at once with dogma, ethical theory, and political theory. I cannot promise such adequacy, but perhaps an inadequate initial attempt may be useful.

There are, it seems to me, three subquestions—or there are three if the first two are answered as I will propose. The first is, *Can* differences about ethics be properly church divisive? We may, I think, limit the field for immediate discussion; the most obvious candidates for such a role will be questions that either determine church discipline—for example, must a bishop really be the husband of no more than one wife?—or questions on which churches will make a witness whether they want to or not—for example, can there be a right to abort an unborn child? Or what military actions are just, if any?

The question is not whether differences about ethics in fact divide the church; they have done so throughout history and are doing so now with new virulence. The question is whether some such divisions are unavoidable—whether, faced with an ethical disagreement that at least for the foreseeable future cannot be reconciled, it can in some cases be necessary for one party to recognize that for that same foreseeable future it cannot be in complete eucharistic and ministerial fellowship with the other party.

The second question supposes an affirmative answer to the first: Supposing that divisions in ethics sometimes truly divide the church, how do we tell when that is the case? What are the criteria? If, as seems likely, some ethical divisions are tolerable within communion and some are not, how do we tell the difference? And the third question is, When it appears that some of us cannot for reasons of ethics be in full fellowship with others whom we nevertheless regard as church, what are we to do about that?

Can It Happen?

The dominant voices of the contemporary American church say that disagreement about ethics cannot be legitimately church divisive. It is widely said—especially at the headquarters of the once-mainline Protestant denominations—that such disagreements cannot break our "unity in Christ" and that this "deep" unity mandates "living together" despite being unable to agree about major points of church discipline or of moral witness to the world.

Now at some level this must be right. Those baptized into Christ are indeed bound together in a bond that can be broken only by deliberately renouncing it—and perhaps even explicit renunciation cannot finally succeed. But just what level is it where this bond obtains?

I will argue that the unbroken unity in Christ of baptized believers divided in moral discipline or public moral witness obtains at the *same* level as does the unity of baptized believers divided in doctrine. In the case of doctrinal division, the contradiction between broken fellowship and deep unity in Christ is the very motive of ecumenical dialogue. That doctrinally separated communities of the baptized are nevertheless somehow one in Christ is a mandate to *argue* the differences, not permission simply to live with them. Indeed, this shared effort is itself a necessary part of their remaining unity. Just so, I propose, the contradiction between "unity in Christ" and division about what sorts of sexual behavior are blessed, for example, is a mandate for something much like traditional ecumenical dialogue, not permission to live with the dissensus. And the necessity of that effort is again an essential part of remaining unity in Christ.

So to the argument. That matters of ethics have in fact divided the church, and that such divisions have in fact often been taken as holding at the same level as divisions caused by doctrine, is a matter of open record.

Thus the canons of the ancient councils are very much about ethics. Studying them in seminary—if indeed we still do—we skip over those bits, but the councils themselves lay down their ethical judgments right along with their doctrinal judgments. A canon of the very first ecumenical council, at Nicea, offers a nice example. There was at the time a self-segregated sect of rigorists that prohibited second marriages, at least by clergy. Some bishops and presbyters of the sect were applying for re-entry into the clergy of the catholic church. The council decreed that they were to be admitted, but only after making formal renunciation of this rule. One could not, according to the council, advocate a prohibition of second marriage and be in the communion of the catholic church.

For a more recent case, one may instance the Lutheran World Federation's break of fellowship with the white Lutheran churches of South Africa, on account of their practice of apartheid. The action was widely applauded at the time—including by some who now call for living together in spite of almost anything. The Lutheran churches trotted out the heavy artillery, *status confessionis*: tolerating apartheid was held to contradict the church's confession of faith. And then one may note Second Peter's vehement exclusion from all fellowship of a party whose fault, so far as it can be made out, was their tolerated sexual practices.

Now of course it could be maintained that the historical fact that the church has often treated some ethical disagreements as breaking fellowship in the same way as do some doctrinal disagreements, does not in itself prove that this *ought* to have been done—though surely it imposes some burden of proof on those who maintain the contrary. What will surely settle the matter are instances of recognized necessary teaching that simply are *at once* doctrinal and ethical. Are there any? It seems to me that there are indeed. And of course what I really want is scriptural instances; something from the New Testament would be very nice.

So consider Paul's argument in 1 Corinthians 11:17ff. The problem in Corinth was the way in which more prosperous believers treated the less prosperous at the common meals of which the eucharistic loaf and cup were then a part. It was a mandate recognized throughout the earliest church, not as an ideal but as a rule of church discipline: the economically well-off are to share with the less well-off. And of course the paradigm of such care was the sharing of food at the bonding meal of the ecclesia. Indeed, in the first Jerusalem congregation, as Luke tells it, certain necessities of life were administered from a common chest—an ethic enforced in one case of dereliction and a cover-up by a particularly final sort of excommunication.

Paul finds some Corinthians in violation of this discipline. How does he deal with it? He does not repeat and emphasize the rule, nor does he enforce it from general ethical principles of generosity or even from the law of God—though elsewhere he can do that sort of thing perfectly well. Instead, he invokes the doctrine of the risen Christ's bodily presence *for* the church and *as* the church: the errant Corinthians by their defiance of the rule of sharing violate the Corinthian assembly's unity as the body of Christ, and just so they violate Christ's body on the table. Now, that the shared bread and wine are the one body of the risen Christ, and that just so the community that shares them is the same one body of the risen Christ, is surely a piece of doctrine if there ever was one (and indeed an especially challenging one), and Paul makes it the warrant for his rebuke of certain Corinthians' ethical deviation.

Of course, in prophetic style, Paul wants the Corinthian offenders to repent. What if they refuse? Paul apparently then even expects some of them to depart the church by the same route as Annanias and Saphira. And if the delinquents were to defy Paul's ruling by starting their own eucharistic fellowship, where they could divide their goods according to their own reasonings about justice and propriety, would not that be schism? One can imagine the Corinthians' position: the Lord has given us these goods. Would he have done that had he not wished us to enjoy them, in or out of the ecclesia? Or if the prosperous packed a meeting, took over the Corinthian congregation, and established their own ethic of appropriate stewardship, would not Paul have called the faithful to come out?

The most profound and obvious case in which biblical doctrine and biblical ethics are inextricably entangled is also the case that is currently most distressing the churches. There is no way for me to avoid the matter of marriage. Can disagreement about who can be married, and the subplots of that argument, constitute a break of church fellowship?

I need to start with the word itself. *Marriage* and its equivalents in other languages have heretofore functioned as a *label*—not as a concept, but as a mere label—for the legal and cultural forms by which societies recognize and regulate a particular biological-social phenomenon, one that is simply found to be there. That phenomenon is the coincidence of the most complete possible bodily union between existing human persons, with equally bodily unity between old and new human persons. *Marriage* was a label for the culturally and legally recognized unity of ordered sexual passion and ordered procreation, for the culturally and legally recognized forms of that bio-social phenomenon in which the two constituting modes of human society, synchronic unity at one time and diachronic unity across time, occur as one relation. Thus also in Scripture the word *marriage* and its derivatives do no more than mention an institution that is assumed to be there, and indeed this one.

We should perhaps further note that in its previous use, the word *marriage* did not specify a mode of affection or of personal commitment, though these have often been counted as blessings of marriage, and may well come to be the most treasured part of the relation. But persons could be in the relation labeled *marriage* with or without notable affection or private commitment. If we wish to talk about the reality previously labeled *marriage*, we will not regard these blessings as the constitutive aspects of the relation.

These matters noted, let me for a while drop discussion of the word *marriage* and directly consider the phenomenon heretofore so labeled. The Scriptures interpret the phenomenon in their very first statement about what it means to be human. According to Genesis, God creates *ha-adam*, "the Adam" in the singular—with the article, not a personal proper name—*as* "male and female" in the plural. This striking proposition presents itself as what Western philosophy would call an "ontological" proposition. That is to say, it describes a fundamental structure of human being: to be human is to be one of a possible pair, to be male or female, to have an other that is made other by correlated bodily difference. To quote an aphorism devised or borrowed by an able student of mine last semester, "Humanity is male *and* female; each human is male *or* female." Nor should we dismiss the first creation narrative as myth or legend. As historical scholarship has long since made clear, it is the product of a philosophically and scientifically sophisticated scholar-priest, or perhaps of a school of such savants, who knew exactly what he or they were doing.

Then, in the second creation account, we are told how this unity-in-duality is actual: a man leaves his parents and "cleaves" to his wife, and the two become one *basar*, "one flesh," as it is usually translated. This word *flesh*, as it functions in the Old Testament, is complex. To begin, something that is flesh is anything that is real but is not God, that is to say, a creature. Thus "all flesh is as grass" simply means that all creatures are as perishable as is the creature grass. But *flesh* further denotes the sheer stuff of living creatures—from leaves of grass to advanced organs—that in fact distinguishes them from God.

Each half of the couple is depicted as flesh as the other is flesh, in the most direct fashion: they were once a single chunk of it. These two, the man and the woman, then come together by the mutually adapted flesh of their bodies, to be one real new creature, one flesh, precisely by the pairing of their organs.

Now it might be argued that this biblical ontology is not directly Christian doctrine; after all, we are not compelled to adopt the science of the creation accounts, why should we adopt their ontological views? But that escape is stopped by New Testament Christology.

At a famous passage in Ephesians (5:31–32), the author quotes our passage from Genesis. Then he interprets: "This passage tells a deep mystery; here I read it of Christ and the church." Is he interpreting the mystery of sexual union by the relation of Christ and the church, or the mystery of Christ and the church by sexual union? Perhaps the final exegetical judgment must be that he is doing both at once. But the context makes the first interpretation primary, and that is anyway the one that concerns us.

Read in context, the passage could not be plainer: the author of Ephesians founds the unity of husband and wife by the unity of Christ and the church. Note that he does not do this by analogy or anything of that sort; he does not say that the union of male and female is *like* that between Christ and the church. That Christ and the church are together one real thing, and that spouses together are one real thing, are in the text a *single* mystery that can be read in the two contexts. A systematic treatment of this profound christological ontology would take us well beyond the bounds of this essay; acknowledging that it obtains is all we need here.

The account in Genesis 2 may date from a time when polygamy was still at least tolerated in Israel. Yet it presumes a couple as the new one thing created by male-female cleaving. The reason why monogamy became normative for Israel and so for the church should in fact be sufficiently plain from this passage; if it is not, the Ephesians passage nails it down: there is one woman and one man in the new one flesh *in that* there is one Israel and one divine Bridegroom, one church and one Christ; both unities are aspects of the same mystery. In the Old Testament, for Israel to cleave to a god beside the Lord is "whoring"; *just so* for a spouse to cleave to another beside the one spouse came to be understood as transgression—as it has not been understood by most of humanity.

Finally, Genesis specifies a mission for the couple. They are to be God's stewards of his creation, and to enable this they, like the rest of animate creation, are to be fruitful and multiply, so as to populate the earth through time. Therewith we arrive at the phenomenon labeled *marriage* at the beginning of this section: the union of humanity's synchronic unity with its diachronic unity, of the bodily unity of two existing human persons with the bodily unity of successive human persons. And therewith we have also the reason why all intact societies have recognized this phenomenon as essential to the existence of society and have therefore regulated it legally and by custom. It is the place where the two societally constituting modes of social unity coincide, and do so in the flesh we—willy-nilly—are.

Now, what about that label for such regulation, the word *marriage*? Plainly, a use of the noun *marriage* paired with, for example, *same-sex* has no overlap at all with its historical use. Much public discourse about *marriage* does not notice that, and thus is mere babble; *The New York Times'* editorial discussions of the matter seem to be produced by someone who would think that the use of the vocable *ball* both for a spherical toy and for a formal dance must indicate some common essence.

But if the culture of the world decides in its own discourse to abolish the label's previous use, there is not much the church can do about it. Maybe it will have to find a new label for the ontological fact affirmed in Christian doctrine. Anyway, the churches within their own discourse must reckon with what the word *marriage* now denotes—or rather fails to denote—for many others, and not allow their own discourse to be confused by mere linguistic mishap. We need to rule for our own discourse: what the world (or much of the world) now means by *marriage* is not what we mean by it—if indeed we are to continue using the word at all.

And if one churchly party goes with secular society in its new labeling, and thereby suggests that same-sex and paired-sex unions are the same sort of thing, and another party denies it, their unity as church is at very least deeply compromised. For disagreement about the ontological status of what was once called *marriage* is simultaneously an ethical and a doctrinal disagreement: it is a disagreement about a fundamental structure of human being as Scripture describes it, a structure established in Christ's relation to the church.

So far as the world outside the church is concerned, the one party to such a disagreement must testify that a society that does not privilege what used to be called *marriage*—under whatever label—is doomed to disintegration, though its outward unity may perhaps be maintained by force or deception. For the institution that unites the society's synchronic coherence with its diachronic coherence will have been abolished. While I am at it, however, let me say that confusing same-sex and opposite-sex pairings, by putting them under the same label, is only the latest and perhaps not most decisive manifestation of our society's continuing suicidal attack on its constituting institutions.

Now, let us suppose two churchly parties who present contrary witness to the world in this matter. Would not at least one of them be what one might call ethically heretical?

How Do We Tell?

If, as in all intuitive likelihood is the case, there are ethical disagreements that do damage church fellowship and others that do not, how do we tell the difference? And let me ask any readers who are unpersuaded by my answer to the first question simply to treat the following as analysis of a problem they do not have, and perhaps enjoy my struggles with it.

Instances where ethical division is churchly division are surely not limited to those that like the above examples present an identity of ethical and doctrinal consensus or dissensus. These establish the possibility that ethical disagreements can divide at the same level as do doctrinal disagreements. But that possibility once established, I think we must expect church-divisive ethical disagreements also where there is no strict identity of ethics and doctrine. How do we discover those?

Let me make a shocking suggestion: we might do well by using the Ten Commandments as our criterion. For in Scripture these play a dual role. They are direct and blunt proclamations of God's covenant with his people. And just so they function as axioms for quite detailed structures of communal ethics and law.

That according to Jesus and Deuteronomy, loving God and the neighbor summarizes the commandments does not mean that the dual commandment replaces them. The dual commandment precisely *summarizes* them. If then we want to unpack what the dual commandment *means* by "love," the move will be in the other direction: to love God and the neighbor means to behave as the two tables lay down.

Now to the pivot of this argument. Within the whole body of the "statutes and ordinances" that are to guide the life and mission of the people of God, Scripture gives the Ten Commandments a unique and specifically theological position. They are spoken "face to face" by God to the people, and not through the mediation of Moses, as are the rest—thus they do not fall within Paul's critique of commandments given by a mediator. God himself then writes them in stone. And, decisively for their doctrinal status, those stones were the chief contents of the ark of the covenant, that is, they were the place of God's saving presence with his people.

It is therefore entirely in accord with Scripture when Martin Luther—so often mistaken for a prophet of American antinomianism—says in his Large Catechism that the whole purpose of the gospel is to enable *Lust und Liebe zu alle Gebote Gottes*, "Eros and agape for all God's commandments"—by which last phrase he explicitly means the ten he has just finished expounding.

As Luther here explains the matter to parents and other teachers of the young, faith in the gospel does not replace or obviate obedience to the Ten Commandments. Instead, it enables us to love obeying them, in the fashion of the psalmists. In his explanations of the second table of commandments, they therefore appear as statements of how we will behave to others *because* we have faith in God. The link between faith in God and love of the commandments is explicit. The explanations of the commandments of the second table, which children were to memorize, all begin, "We should fear and love God so that we . . ."

Of course, interpretation and casuistry always happen between a commandment and a maxim for immediate behavior, and these will always have to be argued out. But there is no mystery about what "adultery" *is*, for example, either in what an historical critic may call the text's "original" import, or in the history of Jewish or Christian interpretation: any sexual act that intrudes on that strange new creature of God, the "one flesh" he creates by bodily union of male and female.

So, a proposed rule: if an act can with some certainty be construed as a violation of one of the commandments, an ethic that recommends it is church-divisive.

So What to Do?

The third question has in turn two parts. There are existing churchly divisions that involve ethical dissensus. And there are situations in which those who once made a single churchly fellowship find their unity threatened by the emergence of ethical dissensus.

With the first sort of division, the mandated course is relatively easy to discern. Churches now separated by different stands on such things as American law about abortion should simply include them on their agenda for dialogue.

With newly emerging division, decisions are trickier. What are people to do who find themselves ethically divided from others with whom they once formed a single ecclesial body? I will be cautious here, since there are several such struggles currently afoot, and I am no longer on the front line.

The question is not primarily about individuals; I carefully spoke of "parties" and "groups" throughout the foregoing. As the moral unity of the American churches collapses, every individual's problem will be specific, and as individuals we will each just have to muddle through.

But ecclesially, I fear, formal schism will sometimes be the result. If the libertarian Corinthians had taken over the existing congregation's church order, those who wanted to obey the mandate of care for the poor at the Supper would obviously have needed their own congregation.

But sometimes also, as the structure of the American churches collapses, confusion will be the determining factor. Morally opposed groups may have no alternative but to live with *partly* broken fellowship. In strict logic, eucharistic and ministerial fellowship is either intact or simply broken, but history does not always obey strict logic and neither then does God's providence—or indeed churches' practice, including that of Roman Catholicism.

For a doctrinal instance: Can those who affirm catholic doctrine of the ministry join in a Eucharist celebrated by an unordained person? Certainly not. But need they depart altogether from a denomination that sometimes permits such things? Perhaps not, though the call is close. For an instance of ethical dissensus: Can those who defend the necessity of what used to be called marriage join in moral witness to the world with those who do not? They obviously cannot, and they must raise their voices to make their own witness. But need they immediately depart from a body they deem morally heretical at this point? The call is even trickier.

2

Race, Slavery, and Shattered Churches in Early America

Beth Barton Schweiger

Both read the same Bible, and pray to the same God; and each invokes His aid against the other ... The prayers of both could not be answered—that of neither, has been answered fully. The Almighty has His own purposes.

—Abraham Lincoln, Second Inaugural Address (March 4, 1865)

Lincoln knew whereof he spoke. As a native Kentuckian raised in the backwoods of southern Indiana and the empty reaches of central Illinois among people with primitive Baptist inclinations, he had the cadence of Scripture drilled into him deeply enough to shape nearly everything he wrote. Lincoln was a product of an American culture that was rooted in Scripture. The American Revolution had undermined trust in other kinds of traditional authority, and confidence in the Bible, and in the ability of ordinary readers to understand it, only grew in Lincoln's lifetime. Publishing and distribution of the Bible dwarfed all other literary enterprises in the young nation. All of these Bibles were needed because about 40 percent of the nation's population claimed formal membership or close affiliation with evangelical Protestant churches in the decades before the Civil War, with an additional 7.5 percent (and rapidly growing) Roman Catholic. So almost half of the nation's population claimed church membership. These numbers, while impressive, do not tell the entire story. The number of people who participated regularly in churches was likely twice that of those who held formal membership. (By contrast, today only about half of those who claim formal membership even attend church.) Christianity, mainly evangelical Protestantism, formed the largest and most formidable subculture in nineteenth-century American society.

These American Christians began killing each other on the battlefield in 1861. By the time Lincoln delivered his inaugural four years later, more than seven hundred thousand people (civilians and soldiers) were dead. In this essay, I want to briefly tell the story of how slavery became the source of this deadly conflict between Christians, one that was ultimately solved by armies rather than by arguments. After almost two millennia of tolerating, and in some cases, defending human slavery, some Christians began to be persuaded that slavery was evil in the eighteenth century. This was an astonishingly new idea, albeit one that gained ground very quickly in an era marked by liberal revolutions that promoted individual rights. Slavery became a political, economic, and social problem in the nineteenth century, but it also became a theological problem—that is, it was a problem for Christians, between Christians, and for their theology. It is the considered opinion of historians that responsibility for those seven hundred thousand deaths lies in large measure with the Church.

This story is actually the story of two divisions within the Church—one over race, the other over slavery. Christians accepted divisions over race long before they began killing each other over slavery. These two issues—race and slavery—cannot be separated from one another. I will frame my remarks with several questions. First, why did slavery become a problem for Christians after they had tolerated it for two millennia? Second, what happened to churches in the United States when it did? Third, what was the relationship between slavery and race in this conflict? And finally, why might all of this matter for us today?

When and Why Did Slavery Become a Problem for the Church?

The world in which Christianity first emerged did not conceive of human slavery as an intolerable evil. Human servitude and bondage had existed in a bewildering variety of forms throughout the ancient world, East and West, and *no authoritative voice from antiquity or during the first centuries of the Church condemned it.* Plato and Aristotle took slavery for granted, as did St. Augustine and St. Thomas Aquinas. In the Christian church, a few voices, such as Gregory of Nyssa, protested against enslavement, but none called for an end to the practice. Slavery was simply assumed. Fundamental to Christian theology was the view that sin and salvation were akin to slavery and freedom. Augustine held that the pain of slave labor was simply the wretched consequence of sin in the City of Man. In this view, the independent, natural human being idealized in the ancient world was a sinner who lacked a capacity for virtue, and thus was enslaved. If she accepted the gift of God's grace, then she would be freed from the slavery of sin. But by accepting the gift, she would become a slave of righteousness. Perfect liberty, then, lay in absolute submission, or enslavement, to God. Thus, Christianity raised obedience, humility, patience, and resignation to the level of high virtues in sharp contrast to the view of the ancients that the servile character was lowly and vicious. It was this sustained connection of slavery to sin, subordination, and the divine order that made questioning the ethical basis of slavery particularly difficult.

But these difficulties began to be surmounted in the eighteenth century. As the great intellectual historian David Brion Davis observed, "For some two thousand years men thought of sin as a kind of slavery. One day they would come to think of slavery as a sin."[1] In light of slavery's long and unremarkable reputation as a natural and necessary thing in the Christian tradition, this remarkable shift from sin as slavery to slavery as sin hardly seemed self-evident. But *the shift did come, beginning in the eighteenth century*. Why?

There are many answers to this question, of course, but fundamentally, slavery became a problem for some Christians because slavery as practiced in the New World was *a new kind of slavery*, unprecedented in human history. New World slavery was a racialized, chattel slave system that offered its African victims only one option: to be enslaved for life and to produce descendants who, if they survived the brutal conditions of their lives, would remain in bondage. The buying and selling of humans on such a grand scale within an intricate and profitable international market that produced staple crops such as sugar, tobacco, and coffee supported a wildly profitable

---

1. David Brion Davis, *The Problem of Slavery in Western Culture* (Ithaca, NY: Cornell University Press, 1966) 90.

system of plantation-based agriculture that stretched from the Portuguese islands off the coast of North Africa to West Africa, westward across the Atlantic from the plantations of Brazil, north to the mines and plantations of Mexico, the hugely profitable plantations in the French, British, Dutch, and Spanish colonies in the Caribbean, north to the indigo and rice plantations in Georgia and South Carolina and the tobacco plantations of North Carolina, Virginia, and Maryland. All in all, between 1500 and 1870, twelve million Africans crossed the Atlantic Ocean, the largest forced migration in human history. Ninety-five percent of these people were bound for slave markets south of the United States.

After the American Revolution, this new kind of slavery became an increasing problem for American Christians. The emerging critique was based in the confluence of Christian theology and Enlightenment ideas of individual liberty. Slaves themselves, some of them freed by British troops during the Revolution, asked for relief. Blacks in Massachusetts petitioned the legislature in 1773 to end the slave trade, and several Puritan ministers circulated letters urging its end. A black abolitionist movement, particularly powerful in Philadelphia and other northern cities, began to print and publish newspapers and pamphlets that argued against slavery. The doctrines of the revolution, summarized in Jefferson's simple phrase "all men are created equal," made slavery increasingly incongruous in a republic devoted to principles of liberty. Some white Christians, particularly in the upper South, began to manumit their slaves as a consequence, creating a new class of black Americans, neither enslaved nor entirely free—free blacks. Quakers had a long tradition of opposition to slavery, and other Christians, black and white, joined their voices. Yet this agitation to end slavery was countered in the early nineteenth century by the emergence of a proslavery Christianity. This argument gained power among slaveholders and theologians in the Southern states, and was supported by clergy in many traditions. Their argument was an explicitly theological one: chattel slavery was not only allowed by God, it was in fact a positive good that benefitted African slaves by exposing them to Christianity and to the civilizing mores of European civilization.

What Happened in the United States?

By the 1830s, these disagreements over slavery began to dominate discussions within denominations. *Denomination after denomination was shattered by the slavery controversy.* The first were the Presbyterians. Although the Old School-New School split in 1837 was not explicitly over slavery, it essentially divided Presbyterians along sectional lines. The Old School dominated the South and held sway at Princeton Seminary under the leadership of theologian Charles Hodge, while the New School prevailed in the North. Old School Presbyterians held to a more continental view of Reformed theology, staunchly opposed revival tactics, and suppressed discussion of the ethics of slavery. The northern-dominated New School split again in 1857, explicitly over slavery, while the Old School split again only after war was declared.

Methodists, in the spirit of John Wesley, were initially antagonistic towards slavery. This stance weakened over time, in large measure because Methodism was a creature of the upper South. The General Conference of 1836 condemned both slavery and "abolitionism," yet by the early 1840s, twelve hundred Methodist ministers owned about fifteen hundred slaves. Antislavery Methodists organized by the early 1840s (Wesleyan Methodists in Michigan, the Wesleyan Methodist Connection in upstate New York). By 1844, there was public opposition to a slaveholding bishop, and after a contentious two-week meeting, northern and southern delegates agreed to part ways; in May of 1845, the Methodist Episcopal Church, South, was formed. Bitter animosity between the two churches prevailed.

Among the Baptists, the story was a bit different because of their congregationalist tradition of government. The primary agency at the national level was the General Convention for Foreign Missions. For a time, it was able to maintain an officially neutral stance on slavery, but by the 1840s, sectional tensions increased over the issue. In 1845, the Southern Baptist Convention was officially organized during a meeting in Augusta, Georgia.

Several churches avoided a split over slavery. Lutherans avoided a formal split largely because the General Synod, which often took an antislavery stand, did not wield strong power, and individual synods were organized in such a way as to squelch open controversy over the issue. The exception was the Franckean Synod in western New York, which organized in 1837 on a strictly antislavery basis. Episcopalians were similarly able to hold together until the Confederacy was established in 1861.

Roman Catholics, meanwhile, never took an official position on the question. Slavery, in the view of the Church, violated neither natural law nor Church teaching. The Church had historically condemned the slave trade, and this was reiterated by Pope Gregory XVI in 1839, when he banned

Catholics from participating in the slave trade but, significantly, not from owning slaves. The American church took no official position on slavery, but opinion in the Church was complicated by the strongly anti-Catholic views of most Americans in this period. Even some of the most radical abolitionists described Catholicism itself as a kind of slavery. All manner of opinions could be found among Irish, German, and French Catholics on the question. Some Catholic liberals, notably Orestes Brownson, staunchly opposed slavery, but virtually none publicly denounced it. More common was the view of editor James McMaster. Like most Catholics, whose acceptance of slavery included racism but did not wholly depend upon it, and who did not see slavery as a "divine right," McMaster saw the issue as a historical one. "There has never been a day in which Catholics, in the communion of the church and uncensured by her, have not held slaves."[2]

Those Protestant denominations that divided bitterly over slavery disagreed about the meaning of the Bible. Lincoln's remark that Yankees and Confederates read the same Bible might have been expanded to include this vital point: *they not only read the same Bible, they read it in exactly the same way.*

This, the historian Mark Noll has brilliantly concluded, is why the debates over slavery within the Church were so bitter and, ultimately, beyond any possibility of resolution short of violence. Noll tells the story of how Protestants in the early United States created a specifically American theology out of three strands: commonsense theism rooted in eighteenth-century Scottish moral philosophy, republican ideology, and evangelicalism (especially Reformed). Most pertinent here is the widespread influence of a commonsense, literal approach to interpreting the Bible. Most American Protestants embraced a language of theistic common sense about 1800, and this approach deeply informed not only traditional theology, but also popular interpretation of the Bible. This commonsense hermeneutic, at heart, fostered a literal reading of Scripture that could *both sanction slavery and condemn it.* And therein lay the problem: American Christians who opposed slavery and those who supported it were reading the same Bible in exactly the same literal, commonsense way. "He who believes the Bible to be of divine authority, believes those laws were given by the Holy Ghost," the proslavery Baptist Thornton Stringfellow wrote in a treatise that he believed proved beyond all doubt the biblical sanction of slavery. "I understand the

2. John T. McGreevy, *Catholicism and American Freedom: A History* (New York: Norton, 2003) 71.

modern abolitionist sentiments to be sentiments of mortal hatred against such laws and which would hold God himself in abhorrence."[3] Yet in 1837, the abolitionist Theodore Dwight Weld published a book called *The Bible Against Slavery*, and used exactly the same hermeneutic approach to come to the opposite conclusion. In 1845, a debate in Cincinnati between two Presbyterians had one proclaiming that the antislavery principle "blazes from every page of God's Book," while his opponent bluntly challenged him to show "from the Bible that the Patriarchs did not hold slaves, that there were no slaves in the apostolic churches, and that the Apostles excluded slaveholders from the Church of God. Let him prove these things and we will give up the question." As in this debate in Cincinnati, proslavery and antislavery readers of the Bible argued to a draw.[4]

There were alternative ways to read the Bible, of course. Non-Reformed Christians such as African Americans, Roman Catholics, Lutherans, and German Reformed all offered an alternative way to read Scripture. None of these, however, was able to eclipse the widespread influence of the literalist approach. There were a variety of reasons for this, but one stands out: Noll shows how the literal reading of the Bible was underwritten by a common-sense consensus about race. In short, white Americans could not separate questions about the Bible and slavery from the Bible and race. In other words, if they found that the Bible sanctioned slavery, they assumed it was black slavery. If they found that the Bible opposed slavery, they assumed it was black slavery. Both opponents of slavery and advocates of slavery assumed that slavery was about people of African origin. They could not tell the difference between slavery and the enslavement of African Americans, so deeply ingrained was black slavery in their culture. Another way to say this is that almost all white readers of the Bible brought assumptions about race and slavery to their reading of the Scriptures. The power of their assumptions is revealed in the simple observation that if slavery was in fact sanctioned by God, then it might have been good for a wide variety of people to be enslaved. Yet, not even the staunchest defender of slavery could ever have imagined that the Bible sanctioned enslaving white people.[5]

3. Thornton Stringfellow, *Scriptural and Statistical Views in Favor of Slavery* (Richmond, 1856) 31.

4. Mark A. Noll, *America's God: From Jonathan Edwards to Abraham Lincoln* (New York: Oxford University Press, 2002) 389, 391–92.

5. Ibid., 417–21.

What Is the Relationship between Race and Slavery in Christian Churches in This Period?

So, it is abundantly clear from these debates that slavery was only part of the problem for nineteenth-century Christians. They were also troubled by questions of race. In fact, within the church, divisions along racial lines long preceded divisions over slavery. The term *racism* did not come into use in the United States until the 1930s. Yet the ability of racial prejudice to twist human action into perverse shapes has long been acknowledged. Many of the most outspoken advocates for emancipation continued to hold racist views of the most virulent kind by today's standards. Opposition to slavery and advocacy of racial equality were two very different positions. Only a handful of Americans achieved the latter. Abraham Lincoln's ambivalent views reflected those of most of his northern peers. An unequivocal opponent of the expansion of slavery into the western territories in the years before the Civil War, Lincoln nevertheless spurned the idea that African Americans were the intellectual equals of European Americans.

Historians have long puzzled over the relationship between race and slavery. Which came first? Did one produce the other? The question remains unresolved, in part, I suspect, because it is too simplistic. *For American Christians, the importance of racial distinctions was evident from the beginning.* This was particularly true after the conversion of large numbers of African Americans (mainly slaves) in the evangelical revivals sometimes called "the First Great Awakening" in the eighteenth century. For the first time, large numbers of people of African origin, both those just arrived from Africa and those who had labored in slavery for several generations in North America, professed Christianity in very large numbers. From the time they embraced Christianity, people of African heritage desired to meet together, apart from white masters, to worship. The earliest recorded black church in what became the United States gathered in Silver Bluff, South Carolina, twelve miles from Savannah, Georgia, in the early 1770s. Black congregations gathered throughout the revolutionary period in the late eighteenth century, driven by a desire to worship God in their own way, as well as by the need to escape the tight supervision and condescension of whites. Gifted black preachers arose in this era, some of them able to gather independent congregations from Portsmouth, Virginia, to Baltimore and elsewhere. Methodists, Presbyterians, and Baptists began to meet, although virtually all had white supervision of some kind. Black Catholics gathered

to worship in St. Augustine, Florida, in the 1780s. All of these developments suggest that both black and white Christians saw *division of churches
along racial lines as natural and necessary as division along doctrinal lines.*

And racial difference was increasingly naturalized in the early decades
of the nineteenth century. This was prompted by several developments.
First, so-called scientific racism was advocated by leading scholars. People
of African ancestry were frankly judged by the best science of the day to be
unarguably inferior to those of European ancestry. Second, white American Christians bolstered theories of racial difference with their proslavery
arguments. Proslavery Christianity was not exclusively a southern view.
Many Christians in the north had few, if any, qualms about black slavery.
Chief among their arguments was the view that Africans were fit for slavery
because they interpreted Noah's curse of Canaan, Ham's son, in Genesis 9
as a mandate for the enslavement of Africans. The historian David Brion
Davis has lamented that no other passage in the Bible has had such a foul
influence on human history.[6]

Yet, in addition to pseudoscientific theories about race and biblical
arguments, there was an intensely pragmatic reason for the segregation of
churches in both North and South: black members overwhelmed white
members in many congregations, particularly Baptist and Methodist congregations. Enslaved and free black believers outnumbered whites by huge
numbers.

The example of First Baptist Church in Richmond, Virginia, one of the
most influential congregations in the nation, suggests the *complexities of
racial prejudice, in particular, the importance of class* in dividing free whites
and enslaved blacks in the same congregation.[7] First Baptist, Richmond,
built its first building in approximately 1798, "a small wooden house with a
shed at either end" that reflected the modest status of the biracial congregation. They baptized members in the nearby "Penitentiary Pool," and later
in the city canal. By 1802, the congregation had built a new, larger church
building, low and simple in style, without a steeple. Through additions and
renovations over the next four decades, this building became the largest
assembly hall in antebellum Richmond. About 1836, almost four decades
on, the congregation installed a baptistry in the church, which included a

6. David Brion Davis, *Inhuman Bondage: The Rise and Fall of Slavery in the New
World* (New York: Oxford University Press, 2006) 64.

7. Beth Barton Schweiger, *The Gospel Working Up: Progress and the Pulpit in Nineteenth-Century Virginia* (New York: Oxford University Press, 2000) 42–46.

mechanical pool with rolling floors and dressing chambers. More momentous even than the new baptistry (the congregation had formerly baptized new members in the James River) was the building of a new church a few years later. In 1841, the congregation literally reinvented itself by constructing a new $40,000 house of worship. The imposing structure, built on a prime lot in the center of the city, was designed by the architect who later designed the new dome and wings of the US Capitol building. The severe Greek revival structure contrasted sharply with the simple and modest old church. In a gesture that underscored its humble appearance, the congregation gave the old building to black members, splitting the congregation along racial lines to found the First African Baptist Church.

First Baptist Church, then, segregated its members upon construction of the imposing new building. Key in this decision was the racial makeup of the congregation. In 1800, the church had fifty white members and 150 black members. At the time the congregation segregated, there were 387 white members and more than seventeen hundred black members. Writers in the local press lavished praise on the new building, lauding its exquisite good taste. The sparkling white walls and ceiling set off the deep blue of the pew cushions nicely. A quilted blue damask hanging centered with a brilliant white star graced the front wall, while the Bible rested on a matching damask cushion. The most striking new feature was the practice of selling and renting pews, apparently adopted by the congregation with little controversy; a professional auctioneer sold pews on a late Tuesday afternoon in 1841 for amounts ranging from fifty to five hundred dollars, paid in installments.

The sale of pews completely altered the social context of worship for the formerly biracial congregation. The majority church membership of slaves and free blacks was gone, and the sale of pews imposed a visible social hierarchy on the white worshippers who remained. The segregation of this urban congregation mirrored what was happening across the country in the decades before the Civil War. What should the social and material context of religious life and worship be? At the heart of the dispute was a deep ambiguity as to whether, and how much, refinement was required of Christian people. Arguments appeared in support of both elegant "churches" and plain "meetinghouses." "The great wail is that [renting pews] drive out the poor," a Baptist observed. "Are the houses of God to be erected exclusively for the poor? It is easier and better to seek to raise the poor to a higher level than to bring other more numerous classes to a lower."[8] What was clear, however, was that the presence of large numbers of black members in a congregation that aspired to attract a better class of people was deemed unsuitable. The story of First Baptist, Richmond, suggests that divisions between black and white church members were rooted in racial prejudice, but it also suggests how deep and complex that prejudice was. Racial prejudice, even during slavery, was never a simple matter of skin color. Instead, the segregation of First Baptist Church lay bare how slavery, pseudoscience, interpretation of the Bible, social class, power, money, and culture came together to naturalize racial segregation. It seemed to be the most "natural" thing in the world to separate a congregation along class and color lines.

In a wonderful book, *The Christian Imagination: Theology and the Origins of Race*, Willie James Jennings suggests that the inability of Christians to overcome racial divisions is rooted in what he terms a "diseased social imagination."[9] Christianity, he argues, embraced from the beginning the possibility of transcending ethnic and racial differences. The New Testament tells how Gentiles and Jews overcame their vast differences to come together in the early Church. One day, St. Luke writes, God surprised the Apostle Peter by commanding him to set aside Jewish dietary laws and to embrace a Roman centurion. "God has shown me," St. Peter told the (no doubt puzzled) people gathered in the house of the centurion, Cornelius, "that I should not call any man common or unclean." God surprises us, Jennings says, by himself loving the differences between people. His love holds out the possibility of intimacy between very different people within the body of Christ. Yet, the history of the church has shown repeatedly that Christians have heeded (or disobeyed) this ancient command by enacting violence and even death—"if not of bodies, then most certainly of ways of life, forms of language, and visions of the world." In the nineteenth-century United States, Protestant churches remained almost entirely segregated along racial lines, and were increasingly segregated along class lines, as they are today. Jennings bluntly challenges our generation of Christians to move beyond postcolonial liberal pieties and our superficial commitment to "diversity" to find the antidote for our racial, ethnic, and class divisions in our deepest experience with God. The theologian Miroslav Volf, who

8. Ibid., 45.

9. Willie James Jennings, *The Christian Imagination: Theology and the Origins of Race* (New Haven: Yale University Press, 2010).

witnessed the violence that Catholic Croats and Orthodox Serbs committed against one another in his native Croatia during the 1990s, agrees. Embracing those who are different to us, Volf says, is possible only if, in the name of God's crucified Messiah, we distance ourselves from ourselves. We must deliberately, consciously, and humbly make room for those who are profoundly different. The implication here is that we cannot be complete within ourselves. God lavishly embraces all together in his arms, and we can be complete only in this unity of difference.

Conclusion: Armies, Not Arguments—Why Does This Matter to Us Today?

Willie Jennings offers us one reason why it is important to consider the history of the church of the nineteenth century—a church divided over the issues of race and slavery. "It is not at all clear that most Christians are ready to imagine reconciliation" in the wake of colonialism and racial strife, Jennings writes. Before we can imagine reconciliation, he explains, we "must articulate the profound deformities of Christian intimacy and identity in modernity." Studying the history of the body of Christ is one way to begin to do this. Only after we fully see, unblinkingly, the ways that the Church has fallen short can we begin to address the legacy of those shortcomings in our own generation.

Are there other ways in which remembering this tragic history of division over slavery and race in American churches—a history we surely would rather forget—can be useful to us? Although I am a historian and not a theologian, I'd like to close by briefly suggesting three uses of this particular past for our generation of Christians.

These uses seem straightforward and disarmingly simple. First, good theology matters. It might have gone a very long way towards preventing the deaths of those seven hundred thousand people in the nineteenth century, and might have even prevented the war itself. Theology can save lives. I can testify that theology has saved my own sanity as I work in the midst of an academy that often seems bent on violence, albeit rhetorical rather than physical. Wise and generous theological voices have chastened me of my anger, and have suggested a better way to live among my peers.

Second, contemplating the shortcomings of our ancestors warns us against a glib, teleological view the past. The wrong conclusion to draw from studying how slavery and race divided the church in past generations is that we triumphed over those weaknesses and, thank God, we abolished slavery and passed the Civil Rights Act of 1964. We cannot afford such arrogance. As I tell my students, the failures of our forebears are hardly cause for smug triumphalism. They are instead an opportunity for humility. What can we learn from Christian slaveholders? They teach us to look for the logs in our own eyes. Christian slaveholders were blind to the enslaved human beings who stood before their eyes. They died unwilling to embrace the full wisdom offered in their theology and unable to breach the terrible chasm that opens when one human being claims complete power over another. They can teach us how easily blindness comes upon human beings. They force us to ask, what are *we* blind to? Who is standing in front of us that we do not see?

And finally, I end where I began. "Both read the same Bible and prayed to the same God," Lincoln intoned in the dark and bloody spring of 1865. He himself would fall at the hands of his enemies within the month. The bloody division between Christians over slavery and race in the nineteenth century was a failure of hermeneutics. Theologians—and Christians across the nation—used the Bible to support what they already believed. In their arrogance, they were unable to imagine the Jesus that the Gospels imagined. They read the Bible blindly, unwilling and unable to transcend the conventions of thought in their own age. Tragically, the "theological debates over slavery . . . were settled by armies rather than by arguments." This failure reminds us that we need to keep our eyes wide open as we read the Bible. We cannot afford to read blindly. As the theologian Luke Timothy Johnson has suggested, reading Scripture requires risk taking and imagination. We must learn how to live in the world of Scripture, to leap into *its* life instead of demanding that Scripture reflect our own. We need to imagine the world that the Scriptures imagine, one in which the intimacy and unity of the body of Christ is affirmed.

3

Doctrine: Knowing and Doing

Frederick Christian Bauerschmidt

I

I recall seeing, a number of years ago, a photograph taken in the late 1960s of a Mass concelebrated by Lutheran pastors and Catholic priests. The priests were, of course, Jesuits. Behind the concelebrants was a banner with the slogan, "Doctrine divides; service unites."[1] For me, this image captures a moment in history—a moment of particularly groovy sideburns, but also a moment of intense ecumenical optimism rooted in the idea that the disputes that had divided the Church in the sixteenth century could, in the twentieth century, be set aside in light of the overwhelming consensus among Christians on the pressing issues of the day: civil rights, the elimination of poverty, and world peace. It is an image that expresses what Bernard Lonergan said, in a much more sophisticated way, when he wrote in 1972 that the division among Christians "resides mainly in the cognitive meaning of the Christian message. The constitutive meaning and the effective meaning are matters on which most Christians largely agree. Such agreement, however, needs expression and, while we await common cognitive

---

1. This is a dictum originally coined in 1922 by the German jurist and theologian Hermann Paul Kapler, according to Archbishop Nathan Söderblom in his 1930 Nobel Peace Prize lecture. See "The Role of the Church in Promoting Peace," in *Peace*, ed. Frederick W. Haberman (Singapore: World Scientific Publishing, 1999) 2:106.

agreement, the possible expression is collaboration in fulfilling the redemptive and constructive roles of the Christian church in human society."[2] In other words: doctrine divides (at least for the moment); service unites.

It was an optimistic moment not simply in the dialogue among divided Christians but also, perhaps especially for Roman Catholics, in the dialogue between the Church and the modern world. It was a moment captured in the Second Vatican Council's Pastoral Constitution *Gaudiam et spes*, in which the Church, recognizing that it could never find common ground with modernity on the question of God, turned instead to the question of humanity. The Council Fathers introduced the Constitution by noting, "it is around humankind therefore, one and entire, body and soul, heart and conscience, mind and will, that our whole treatment will revolve." They went on to say that the Council "offers the human race the sincere cooperation of the church in working for that universal community of sisters and brothers which is the response to humanity's calling."[3] Even in dialogue with the modern world, where doctrine divides, service unites, and thus the Pastoral Constitution offered in its second half a series of reflections on the "urgent problems" of the world of today: "marriage and family, human culture, socio-economic and political life, union within the family of nations, and peace."[4] The Pastoral Constitution does not ignore the theological and, particularly, the christological grounding of the Church's position with regard to these urgent problems.[5] One might, however, be forgiven for thinking that, at least for the time being, the common ground between the Church and the world was not to be found in common profession of belief but rather in the common service that would address these urgent problems. Doctrine divides; service unites.

Such a view presumes, of course, a high degree of moral consensus among Christians and between Christians and non-Christians, a consensus that seemed particularly robust in the post–World War II era. I suspect that in Europe that consensus was a result of residual Christian social values combined with the post-Shoah revulsion against totalitarianism that was

2. Bernard Lonergan, *Method in Theology* (Minneapolis: Seabury, 1972) 368.

3. *Gaudium et spes*, preface §3, in *Decrees of the Ecumenical Councils*, ed. Norman Tanner (Washington: Georgetown University Press, 1990) 2:1070.

4. See *Gaudium et spes*, part 2, introduction §46, in ibid., 1100.

5. In particular the first half of *Gaudium et spes* makes clear that the anthropological starting point must terminate in Christ. In the phrase much quoted by John Paul II, "it is only in the mystery of the Word incarnate that light is shed on the mystery of humankind" (*Gaudium et spes*, part 1, ch. 1 §22, in ibid., 1081).

shared by Christians of all stripes, as well as by many non-Christians. In the United States, it was a result of a fairly robust civil religion that was in fact a form of deracinated Protestantism into which Catholics and Jews were being assimilated, a civic religiosity that was nicely summed up by President Eisenhower when he said, "our government has no sense unless it is founded in a deeply felt religious faith, and I don't care what it is."[6] Whatever the source of the consensus, it was clear well into the 1960s to people of differing religious confessions that certain things, like the civil rights movement, were good, and certain other things, like the war in Vietnam, were bad. Of course, the goodness and badness of these things are, at least in popular perception, much easier to judge in hindsight, for as much as Christians were united across doctrinal lines by these moral issues, they were also divided by them. What was significant at the time, however, on a symbolic level, was the sight of Catholic priests and nuns marching in Selma, Alabama, with Martin Luther King, or the key roles played by Fr. Daniel Berrigan, Rev. William Sloane Coffin, and Rabbi Abraham Joshua Heschel (not to mention Richard John Neuhaus) in the founding of Clergy and Laymen Concerned About Vietnam. Here could be seen vividly the way in which consensus on the great moral issues of the day could bridge the divide created by creeds.

Of course, things look a bit different today. Indeed, to some it might seem, in light of theological agreements like the Roman Catholic and Lutheran *Joint Declaration on the Doctrine of Justification* or the World Council of Churches' document on *Baptism, Eucharist and Ministry*, on the one hand, and the divisions within Christian denominations along culture war party lines, on the other, that it is now doctrine that unites and service (or at least ethics) that divides. The neuralgic questions dividing Christians seem no longer to be whether righteousness is forensic or intrinsic, or whether Christ is present in the Eucharist through transubstantiation, sacramental union, virtual presence, or simply our act of remembering. Rather, they are questions of the role of women in church and society, or of the moral status of embryos and how this should shape public policy, or of the acceptance of homosexuality as normal and healthy that have Christians pitted against one another.

---

6. For a source-critical analysis of this Eisenhower *logion*, see Patrick Henry, "'And I Don't Care What It Is': The Tradition-History of a Civil Religion Proof-Text," *Journal of the American Academy of Religion* 49 (1981) 35–49. Henry argues that, seen in context, Eisenhower's statement is not as vapid as it may at first seem.

I would like to suggest, however, that this shift from doctrine to morals—from knowing to doing—is more apparent than real. Specifically, it was true in the past and remains true today that knowing and doing are mutually implicating. So-called doctrinal disputes about belief are equally disputes about the shape of the lives of those who hold those beliefs, while so-called moral disagreements often imply differing systems of belief in which particular moral positions are embedded. As Charles Sanders Peirce put it, "to be deliberately and thoroughly prepared to shape one's conduct into conformity with a proposition is neither more nor less than the state of mind called Believing that proposition."[7] To believe a doctrine is to be prepared to act in a certain way; and our readiness to act in certain ways is attendant upon a network of beliefs.

II

Before looking at a specific example to illustrate this point, I should like to say a bit more about my own particular understanding of terms like "morals" and "ethics." Though I do not subscribe to the view that etymology is equivalent to definition, I do think it instructive to ponder the roots of "moral" in the Latin *mos* and of "ethics" in the Greek *ēthos*, both of which mean "custom." It would be a mistake to draw from this the lesson that morals are simply a matter of custom or convention, but I do think it is true that our moral sense—our sense of whom to praise and whom to blame, of which goods to pursue and which to avoid—derives from a complex web of specific beliefs, institutions, practices, social habits and so forth that might be described as constituting a "moral ecology."[8] Moral norms can only be fully intelligible and convincing in the context of a "culture," which Clifford Geertz defined as "an historically transmitted pattern of meanings

7. "A Neglected Argument for the Reality of God," in *Collected Papers of Charles Sanders Peirce*, ed. Charles Hartshorne and Paul Weiss (Cambridge: Harvard University Press, 1935) 6:467.

8. On "moral ecology" see Allen Hertzke, "The Theory of Moral Ecology," *The Review of Politics* 60:4 (1998) 629–59. Pope Benedict XVI speaks of a "human ecology" in his encyclical *Caritas in Veritate*, noting, "Just as human virtues are interrelated, such that the weakening of one places others at risk, so the ecological system is based on respect for a plan that affects both the health of society and its good relationship with nature. . . . The book of nature is one and indivisible: it takes in not only the environment but also life, sexuality, marriage, the family, social relations: in a word, integral human development" (§51).

embodied in symbols, a system of inherited conceptions expressed in symbolic forms by means of which men communicate, perpetuate, and develop their knowledge about and attitudes toward life."[9] This rooting of morality in culture need not, as some have feared, commit one to "cultural relativism."[10] What it does commit one to, however, is abandoning any clear delineation between "moral" matters and all of the other elements that go into creating the culture or ecology in which questions of the goodness or badness of human actions find their intelligibility.[11] As with a natural eco-system, a moral ecology cannot be engineered, with elements eliminated or introduced willy-nilly, though it may of course undergo incremental change.[12]

9. Clifford Geertz, *The Interpretation of Cultures* (New York: Basic, 1973) 89. Talal Asad has criticized this definition of culture as being focused too narrowly on "con-sciousness" and thus excluding the material conditions of such consciousness. When this definition is then applied to religion as a cultural system, it skews our understanding of religion in an individualist and interiorized direction, and obscures the workings of power in the transition from discourse to action, from cognition to behavior. It seems to me that part of what is at work in Asad's criticisms is a Nietzschean/Foucauldian presup-position against any universal claim or definition and a fascination with "power" as the occluded *tertium quid* linking religious discourse and religious practice. Yet this appeal to "power" seems no less vague and no less universalizing than Geertz's appeal to "cul-ture" or "religion." That being said, Asad offers a salutary reminder that the connection between knowing and doing, while intimate, is not entirely seamless, and that particular social configurations do have a role in "authorizing" both beliefs and behaviors. See Ta-lal Asad, "Anthropological Conceptions of Religion: Reflections on Geertz," *Man*, New Series, 18:2 (1983) 237–59.

10. Geertz himself notes that "the notion that the essence of what it means to be human is most clearly revealed in those features of human culture that are universal rather than in those that are distinctive to this people or that is a prejudice we are not necessarily obliged to share. . . . it may be in the cultural particularities of people—in their oddities—that some of the most instructive revelations of what it is to be generically human are to be found" (*Interpretation of Cultures*, 43).

11. This view was argued, somewhat obliquely, in Elizabeth Anscombe's classic 1958 essay, "Modern Moral Philosophy," in *The Collected Philosophical Papers of G. E. M. Ans-combe* (Oxford: Blackwell, 1981) 3:26–42. It has been robustly developed by Alasdair MacIntyre in, *inter alia*, *After Virtue*, 2nd ed. (Notre Dame: University of Notre Dame Press, 1984); *Whose Justice? Which Rationality?* (Notre Dame: University of Notre Dame Press, 1988); and *Three Rival Versions of Moral Inquiry* (Notre Dame: University of Notre Dame Press, 1990).

12. Also, unlike a natural ecosystem, a moral ecology is almost wholly determined by human choices. Thus the organic metaphor ought not be taken as anything more than a metaphor, such that we forget that decisions about faith and morals are always matters of human agency, even if that agency is an instrument of the Holy Spirit.

One ought not, therefore, separate too easily matters of belief from matters of behavior, matters of doctrine from matters of morality. Of course, one might protest that such a separation is precisely something that Christianity, and the Western intellectual tradition in general, has always done. For example, Aristotle, and following him Thomas Aquinas, distinguished between intellectual and moral virtues.[13] As Thomas makes clear, this distinction grows at least in part from the phenomenon, known to St. Paul no less than to Aristotle, of moral weakness, in which knowing the good does not always equal doing the good.[14] Conversely, this distinction can also explain how someone might be a good biologist or accountant—that is, possess certain intellectual virtues—without being a good human being. Yet even within the tradition that distinguishes intellectual virtues from moral virtues, it is clear that there is a profound connection among all the virtues. For Thomas, perfect possession of any moral virtue requires the possession of all the other moral virtues, in particular prudence, which itself is something of a hybrid between a moral and an intellectual virtue.[15] And the moral virtues themselves are not truly and perfectly virtuous apart from the infused gift of charity, which in turn cannot exist apart from faith, which is a virtue perfecting the intellect.[16] Indeed, Thomas calls faith the first of the virtues and says that "there are no real virtues unless faith be presupposed."[17]

The unity of knowing and doing is perhaps best captured in Thomas's discussion of the gift of wisdom, which is the gift that corresponds to the virtue of charity, and therefore has its cause in the will, while having the intellect as its subject, thus being both speculative and practical.[18] It is precisely this unity of the speculative and the practical that finds expression in the unique structure that Thomas gives to the *Summa theologiae*, in which the discussion of what later would be called "moral theology" is situated within doctrinal reflection: on the one side, discussion of the nature of God, one and triune, as well as creation, and on the other side, Christology

13. Aristotle, *Nichomachean Ethics* 1.13 1103a; Thomas Aquinas, *Summa theologiae* 1–2.58.2.

14. See Rom 7:14–20.

15. *Summa theologiae* 2–2.47.1.

16. See *Summa theologiae* 1–2.65 for one of Thomas's discussions of the connectivity of the virtues.

17. *Summa theologiae* 2–2.4.7.

18. *Summa theologiae* 2–2.45.2, 3.

and eschatology. As Leonard Boyle pointed out a number of years ago, the *Summa* represents a pedagogical experiment on Thomas's part, in which he sought to present the instruction required for the training of Dominican friars in what was one of their most important tasks—the administering of the sacrament of penance—within the context of what was their other most important task—the preaching of Christian doctrine. The identity of Thomas as a Dominican led him to see doctrine and ethics as part of a single task or, to use the metaphor I employed a moment ago, elements within a single ecosystem of knowing and doing. Boyle further notes that the frequency with which the *secunda-secundae pars*—the section of the *Summa* that deals with "practical" matters of virtue and vice—circulated separately from the rest of the *Summa* indicates that Thomas's confreres either didn't understand what he was trying to do, or thought it misguided.[19]

This unity of knowing and doing, of doctrine and ethics, is by no means peculiar to Thomas, or to the Catholic tradition. The other obvious example of a unified treatment of doctrine and ethics is Karl Barth's *Church Dogmatics*. Barth's way of speaking about this connection is of course quite different from Aquinas's. We find little talk of virtue and much of divine command, and an explicit rejection of any appeal to natural law. In Barth the connection between knowing and doing is thought of in terms of the revelation of the God who commands. The action of human beings is always a response to God's action, and the fundamental act of God is self-revelation: "The Word of God does not need to be supplemented by an act. The Word of God is itself the act of God."[20] Thus Barth is clear that "the one Word of God is both Gospel *and* Law. . . It is the Gospel which contains and encloses the Law as the ark of the covenant the tables of Sinai."[21] Ethics is therefore a part of dogmatics, and not a separate topic. Barth furthermore recognizes that Thomas, for all the (from Barth's perspective) shortcomings of his approach, is at one with him in locating ethics within theology.[22]

It does seem odd, however, to speak of a "moral ecology"—or any other sort of ecology, for that matter—in connection with Karl Barth. The claim

19. Leonard E. Boyle, OP, *The Setting of the Summa theologiae of St. Thomas* (Toronto: Pontifical Institute of Medieval Studies, 1982).

20. Karl Barth, *Church Dogmatics* 1/1: *The Doctrine of the Word of God*, 143.

21. Karl Barth, *Church Dogmatics* 2/2: *The Doctrine of God*, 511.

22. Barth writes, "It is certainly remarkable that although Thomas's ethics refers unmistakably to an independent basis it is not presented independently of his dogmatics, but in a subordinate position within it" (*Church Dogmatics* 1/2: *The Doctrine of the Word of God*, 783).

31

that knowing and doing are co-implicated in a complex network of specific beliefs, institutions, practices, social habits and so forth seems at odds with what might be called Barth's "occasionalism," the strong emphasis in his theology on the vertical relationship of obedience to the divine command that would seem to undercut any sense of moral growth or development and the need for an environment in which such growth takes place. The unified knowing-doing of the creature seems to exist suspended in midair, in a moment of existential decision which itself hangs suspended from the free speech-act of the electing God. Yet perhaps the starkness of Barth's formulation of the unity of knowing and doing might be read as a correc- tive to any tendency to treat our discussion of moral ecology as something purely natural, as if the beliefs and practices that make up the ecosystem of Christian existence might be understood on a purely anthropological basis. It reminds us that the health of this ecology stands or falls on its rootedness in God's revelation in Christ and on its ongoing cultivation by the Spirit.

Thus both Thomas and Barth, in rather different ways, present the Christian life as a unity of knowing and doing, the speculative and the practical. Thomas has a perhaps more robust account of the "horizontal" dimension of the interwoven web of beliefs and practices that make up the fabric of the Christian life, whereas Barth offers a perhaps stronger rebuke to any temptation to forget that the Christian life is fundamentally a life of thankful response to God's prior act. But both of them present the knowing and doing of Christians in such an intricately interwoven way that it should forestall the invocation of slogans such as "doctrine divides; service unites," for to separate doctrine and service, faith and works, the speculative and the practical is precisely to unravel the fabric of the Christian life, to frac- ture the ecology of Christian belief and practice.

III

To give a sense of how all of this might be in play in divisions among Chris- tians, I would like to look at an historical example: the case of Augustine and the Donatists in the fourth and fifth centuries. This controversy is notoriously complex, particularly if one takes into account the analogous and historically related controversies involving Cyprian of Carthage and Stephen of Rome in the third century. Aside from historical questions of who did what when, and who took which side and for what reason, there are theological questions of how exactly the positions of the various parties both hang together and relate to each other. By the Middle Ages, and continuing on into the Reformation era, a considerable simplification of the issues involved had taken place: Donatism was identified as a heresy—a deviation of belief—regarding the efficacy of sacraments administered by sinful clergy.[23] It was never entirely lost sight of, however, that the particular question of the sacraments was part of a larger debate over the nature of the Church, and modern historical investigations have brought to the fore once again the complexity of the issues involved.

The Donatist controversy arises from an argument in the North African Church over who would become the bishop of Carthage not long after the end of the Diocletian persecution in 305 AD.[24] To greatly simplify, we might speak of a spectrum of attitudes within the Church with regard to those who had collaborated with Roman authorities under persecution, particularly those Church leaders who had handed over the Scriptures rather than face martyrdom or imprisonment. At one end were the rigorists, who even after the end of the persecution saw their relationship with the authorities as an antagonistic one, and who also took a hard line with those who had compromised during the persecution, in particular the clergy, whom, they argued, should only be readmitted to the Church, if at all, as laymen. At the other end were those who had a less antagonistic attitude toward the Roman authorities and who sought an easier path back into the Church for those who had compromised. Mensurius, who tended toward the latter end of the spectrum, was bishop of Carthage in the immediate aftermath of the persecution, and managed to hold this divided community together. Upon his death, shortly before Constantine issued the Edict of Toleration, Caecilian, who shared Mensurius's general approach, was elected to be his successor in what seems to have been a hotly contested election. Among the many charges that the rigorists subsequently leveled against Caecilian was that one of the bishops who participated in his ordination had collaborated with the Roman authorities during the Diocletian persecution, and therefore the ordination itself was "tainted." They elected Majorinus as the true bishop of Carthage, and thus a schism was born. Majorinus's successor was Donatus, from whom we derive the name "Donatists." The followers of Caecilian called themselves "Catholics,"

23. See, e.g., Thomas Aquinas, *Summa theologiae* 3.64.9 *sed contra*; John Calvin, *Institutes of the Christian Religion*, 4.15.16; *Augsburg Confession* a. 8.

24. For a concise account of Donatism, see Robert A. Markus, "Donatus, Donatism," in *Augustine through the Ages: An Encyclopedia*, ed. Allan D. Fitzgerald, OSA, et al. (Grand Rapids: Eerdmans, 1999) 284–87.

because they saw themselves as representing the consensus of the Church outside of Africa. By the time of Augustine, the chief "doctrinal" issue between the two parties was the Donatist refusal to accept Catholic baptisms as true baptisms, and thus the requirement that converts from Catholicism submit to a second baptism; the Catholics, in contrast, did accept Donatist baptisms. But the issues went far beyond this particular doctrinal point.

The Donatists did not begin from the speculative premise that collaborator-bishops—or those guilty of any other sin, for that matter—were no longer capable of confecting "valid" sacraments. Rather, they were concerned about the purity of the Church, a purity that was at once ritual and moral. They saw themselves as the true heirs of the great North African martyr-bishop Cyprian, who in the mid-third century had led the Church of North African through an analogous conflict in the wake of the Decian persecution. Cyprian writes that "all are absolutely bound to the sin who have been contaminated by the sacrifice of a profane and unrighteous priest."[25] Again, Cyprian writes, "it is manifest that they who are not in the Church of Christ are reckoned among the dead; and another cannot be made alive by him who himself is not alive, since there is one Church which, having attained the grace of eternal life, both lives forever and quickens the people of God."[26] The question was not primarily one of the moral status of the individual minister of the sacraments, but whether or not those sacraments were administered within the ambit of the true Church. And for the Donatists, the true Church—the Church that was the true heir of Cyprian—was the Church of the martyrs and confessors, who had resisted and continued to resist Roman authorities.

When Augustine became bishop of Hippo and began to address the Donatist problem, he realized that the key to winning over the people of North Africa to the Catholic side depended upon being able to claim Cyprian, the venerated martyr-bishop, for his side. As the quotations above indicate, this was no small feat, for Cyprian was unambiguous that there could be no true baptism outside the true Church. In what was either a brilliant insight or a rhetorical sleight of hand, Augustine claimed that while Cyprian had argued against the practice of accepting heretical and schismatic baptisms, his overriding concern was not the purity of the Church, but its unity. He noted that Cyprian was less concerned with moral or doctrinal pollution than he was with the sin of schism—a concern manifested in his refusal to

25. Cyprian, *Epistle*, 67.3. This and subsequent English translations of Cyprian from *Ante-Nicene Fathers*, vol. 5 (Peabody, MA: Hendrickson, 1994).

26. Cyprian, *Epistle*, 70.1.

break communion with Pope Stephen over their disagreement concerning the baptism question.[27] It is true that Cyprian was mistaken on what, in his day, was an undecided issue concerning baptism, but "his error was compensated by his remaining in catholic unity, and by the abundance of his charity."[28] While the Donatists might be Cyprian's descendents in sharing his error, they could lay no claim to his inheritance of unity and love. It was in the context of arguing this larger point that Augustine made his claim that "the baptism of Christ, consecrated by the words of the gospel, is necessarily holy, however polluted and unclean its ministers may be."[29]

IV

Though this is only a sketch of the controversy, it will have to suffice for my purpose, which is to ask, was the Donatist-Catholic schism over doctrinal matters or moral matters? "Donatism," as the name of a heresy, as this name is used in later theological discussions, seems to be a doctrinal position concerning sacramental efficacy. But in Donatism as a historical phenomenon, this specific doctrinal position was a secondary and perhaps tertiary concern. The specific "doctrinal" question of sacramental efficacy was embedded in a host of other sorts of questions that might strike us as "moral" or "ethical" ones. For instance:

- Is it ever acceptable to simulate apostasy by obtaining, either by bribery or forgery, an official certificate testifying that one had sacrificed to the Roman gods? Is it acceptable to simulate apostasy by offering an animal or incense to the gods, if one is not making such an offering sincerely (what the Jesuit casuists of the seventeenth century would call "making a mental reservation")? These are questions that arose in Cyprian's day, during the Decian persecution, and shaped the later perspectives of both Donatists and Catholics.[30]

- Should there be, for certain grave crimes, a permanent exclusion from the Church, an excommunication without remit, a sort of spiritual

27. See Augustine, *On Baptism, Against the Donatists*, 5.25.36. This and subsequent English translations of Augustine from *Nicene and Post-Nicene Fathers*, first series, vol. 4 (Peabody, MA: Hendrickson, 1994).

28. Augustine, *On Baptism*, 1.18.28.

29. Augustine, *On Baptism*, 3.10.14.

30. See the casuistry in which Cyprian engages in works such as *Epistle* 51 or *On the Lapsed*.

capital punishment? Similarly, should Church leaders who have betrayed the Church, if they are readmitted, be permanently barred from all leadership and perpetually marked as *traditores*, perhaps the ecclesial equivalent of being placed on a public sex offender's list (an analogy that, sadly, is particularly striking today)? What, in short, are the limits to forgiveness, and is punishment meant to be a means of rehabilitation or retribution?

- Should violence ever be employed by Christians? In the case of the Donatists, are the insurgents known as *circumcelliones* warranted in their acts of violence against the state-supported Catholic Church? In the case of the Catholics, is the use of the power of the state warranted in defense against the Donatist insurgents? If allowable as a means of defense, is it also justified as a means of coercing the Donatists into the Catholic Church?

In light of these questions, we might be inclined to say that the North African schism was not over doctrinal issues at all, but over moral issues, concerning truth-telling or retribution or violence. These moral issues are certainly weighty ones, and perhaps a blessed relief from the moral issues that currently seem to be dividing churches. But before we decide that the Church-dividing issues in fourth-century North Africa were moral ones, we ought to take a further step back and ask about the broader theological background of these particular issues.

For example, questions of the moral gravity of "simulated" apostasy can only be adjudicated against a background of common assumptions about how interior and exterior acts are related, and of how Christians are called to bear witness, and of what sort of privileged place martyrs have in the Christian imagination. Questions of exclusion and forgiveness are embedded in further questions of divine justice and mercy and of how the relationship between these two is imagined, as well as questions concerning grace and merit and the degree to which the Church was called to purify itself of all corrupt elements. They are also related to exegetical questions concerning, for example, Matt 13:24–30 and whether the Church should be conceived of as the wheat among the tares (the Donatist reading), or as the field that contains *both* wheat *and* tares (Augustine's reading). Likewise, questions of Christians and violence, particularly the violence of the state, perhaps depend upon how one understands the relationship of the thirteenth chapter of Romans to the thirteenth chapter of Revelation, or the relationship of salvation history to world history, or even the relationship of nature and grace.

In short, the long dispute that split the Church in North Africa involved questions about what Christians should do, all of which in turn were only answerable in terms of what the various parties thought that they knew about God and the world. How we act in the world as intentional agents— that is, our distinctively human mode of action—always depends upon how we see the world, upon the possibilities and parameters that present themselves to us. The Donatists, rooted in the North African experience of harsh persecution and the memory of the martyrs, saw a hostile world in which the Church was an enclave of purity that must police its borders in order to remain pure until the day when the lord of the harvest would come to gather the Church into his kingdom. The Catholics, more closely connected to the center of the empire, saw a somewhat more benign world in which the Church was a dynamic force, transforming the world gradually so that eventually God would be all in all. Augustine, who had a foot in North Africa and a foot in the wider world of the Roman Empire, might be seen as offering something of a synthesis of these two worldviews, combining the dynamic, transformative vision of Catholic Christianity with a mitigated form of Donatist dualism, such that the City of God—which is not entirely identifiable with the visible Church—is perpetually on the move, on pilgrimage through history, living cheek by jowl with the earthly city, even within the sacramental bonds of the Church.

It is between these differing visions that disagreements over moral issues take their place. Between Catholics and Donatists there was no significant disagreement over the morality of truth-telling, but there was a difference over the degree to which the Church could accommodate within her bounds those who had failed to bear truthful witness. More striking are the differing attitudes toward Christian use of violent coercion. Some partisans for both sides were willing to countenance the use of violence for certain ends, whether the insurgent violence of the Donatist *circumcelliones* or the state-sanctioned violence employed by the Catholics.[31] The *sort* of violence that each side saw as allowable differed in part, no doubt, because of the coercive force that each had available to it: the Donatists had the widespread popular support that enables insurgent violence, whereas the

31. For a discussion of the variety of Donatist attitudes toward insurgent violence, and the rhetorical strategies of their opponents, see Peter Iver Kaufman, "Donatism Revisited: Moderates and Militants in Late Antique North Africa," *Journal of Late Antiquity* 2 (2009) 131–42.

Catholics had the empire on their side. But it also fit within a particular view of how the Church related to the world. For the Catholics, the Church had the capacity to absorb the world, to transform the empire and even to turn its violence to holy ends. For the Donatists, the Church was to remain apart from the world, the ark of salvation sheltering God's chosen ones from the coming judgment—an ark defended by the blood of the martyrs, but also, perhaps, by insurgent counter-violence. Augustine, again, found himself somewhere in the middle. His understanding of the pilgrim nature of the City of God led him initially to reject the use of coercive state power against the Donatists, but eventually he acceded to a limited use of violence as a legitimate employment of the "peace" of the earthly city. These differences are not differences simply on the question of violence, but rather differences of entire moral or, more generally, theological ecologies.

The conflict over Donatism is sometimes reduced by the sorts of histories of doctrine inflicted on seminarians to a dispute over sacramental efficacy. I hope I have indicated how this sacramental question is embedded within a host of other questions, some of which we might characterize as "moral," such as the question of the legitimacy of the use of violence by Christians. These other questions, in turn, can only properly be understood when seen as part of a larger worldview, a theological "ecology" that shapes not only the answers to our doctrinal and moral questions, but also the very questions that we ask. For Catholics and Donatists to reach a consensus on the question of sacramental efficacy or the moral question of the legitimacy of the use of violence by Christians would have involved a convergence of ecologies, requiring a common thinking through of such things as the meaning of martyrdom, the relation of Church and world, the economies of divine mercy and justice, the role of grace in human transformation, and even the nature of human history itself. In the end, the path of one side suppressing the other proved to be the easier alternative.

V

I think one could give a similar analysis of various other divisive issues in the history of the Church. To take what is probably the most obvious example, the doctrinal reformations of the sixteenth century—both Catholic and Protestant—were part of a wider transformation of the spiritual ecology of early modern Europe. A sense of the complex interplay of belief and practice, doctrine and morals, was pioneered by Max Weber and the much contested thesis of his *The Protestant Ethic and the Spirit of Capitalism*. One might have doubts about his views on the supplanting of ascetic medieval Catholicism by worldly Protestantism, but he was surely correct in trying to draw connections between theological conceptions and practical attitudes, between knowing and doing.[32] More recent revisionist social historians of the sixteenth century, such as John Bossy and Eamon Duffy, have followed Weber's general impulse, if not his specific conclusions, in offering a complex picture, rich in detail, of the transformation of knowing and doing in the early modern period.[33] One cannot grasp the full significance of the reformers' teaching on justification unless one also attends to changing practices regarding liturgy, catechesis, pilgrimage, penance, clerical celibacy, the role of the secular state, usury, almsgiving, and so forth.[34] Nor can one fully appreciate the teaching of Trent on this same question unless one attends to the desire to retain and reform these same practices.[35] The change of one element—whether this is in the realm of knowing or of doing—may well lead to changes within the ecology as a whole.

Thinking of the division of Christendom in the sixteenth century in terms of the development of distinct ecologies can account not just for confessional and moral differences, but also similarities, whether of continuing practices or new developments. The relationships within an ecosystem are

32. See Max Weber, *The Protestant Ethic and the Spirit of Capitalism* [1904/5] (New York: Scribner, 1976).

33. John Bossy, *Christianity in the West: 1400–1700* (Oxford: Oxford University Press, 1985); Eamon Duffy, *The Stripping of the Altars: Traditional Religion in England, 1400–1580* (New Haven: Yale University Press, 1992).

34. Steven Ozment offers a fairly exhaustive list: "Protestants proposed a revolution in religious concepts, practice, and institutions. Even in its modest forms the Reformation called for, and in most Protestant areas permanently achieved, an end to mandatory fasting; auricular confession; the worship of saints, relics, and images; indulgences; pilgrimages and shrines; vigils; weekly, monthly, and annual masses for the dead; the belief in purgatory; Latin worship services; the sacrifice of the Mass; numerous religious ceremonies, festivals and holidays; the canonical hours; extreme unction, confirmation, holy orders, and penance; clerical celibacy; clerical immunity from civil taxation and criminal jurisdiction; nonresident benefices; excommunication and interdict; canon law; episcopal and papal authority; and traditional scholastic education of the clergy" (*The Reformation in the Cities: The Appeal of Protestantism in Sixteenth-Century Germany* [New Haven, CT: Yale University Press] 117–18).

35. David Power emphasizes in particular Trent's concern to articulate a doctrine of eucharistic sacrifice that would secure the practice of offering Masses for particular intentions, as well as the distinctive role of the priest over against the worshipping community. See *The Sacrifice We Offer: The Tridentine Dogma and Its Reinterpretation* (New York: Crossroad, 1987).

so varied and complex that a change in one element might only gradually make its effect felt. Indeed, the very notion of an ecosystem should lead us to expect that we ought to think not in terms of revolutions but of evolutions. For example, despite Luther's grudging acceptance of the practice, attitudes toward divorce changed only gradually. At the same time that Catholicism and Protestantism slowly grew apart in some ways, they were often developing along analogous paths in other ways. John Bossy points out in particular the growth, albeit in different modes, of a more interiorized and individualized approach to Christianity in both Catholicism and Protestantism.[36] This is because the spiritual ecologies of Catholics and Protestants were not sharply divided from each other, nor were they clearly distinguished from the developing ecology of modernity. Despite their doctrinal disagreements, both Catholics and Protestants in the sixteenth and seventeenth centuries were equally subject to such forces as the rise of the nation-state and the development of print culture. Mary Midgely notes that if one thinks of cultures on the analogy of ecosystems then we should expect that different cultures would "shade into one another,"[37] not unlike the way a desert shades into a plain, which in turn shades into a forest. From the center of these ecosystems, the differences might seem quite clear; along the borders, the differences might seem so insignificant that one could pass from one to the other without noticing.

VI

So where does all this leave us with regard to doctrinal and moral divisions within the body of Christ?

First, there ought to be no sharp delineation of the doctrinal and the moral. If, as Peirce said, the state of believing is "to be deliberately and thoroughly prepared to shape one's conduct into conformity with a proposition," then there is something arbitrary about deciding that the presence of Christ in the Eucharist is a doctrinal question while homosexuality is a moral one. Certainly our beliefs about the Eucharist have implications for our actions in the liturgy, but also in the realm of politics.[38] Likewise,

36. Bossy, *Christianity in the West*, 126–40.

37. Mary Midgely, *Can't We Make Moral Judgments?* (New York: St. Martin's, 1991) 90.

38. See, e.g., William T. Cavanaugh, *Torture and Eucharist: Theology, Politics, and the Body of Christ* (Cambridge: Blackwell, 1998).

our views on homosexuality imply and should be informed by our convictions concerning theological anthropology, or the nature of the authority of Scripture, or whether we believe there is a natural law and how we understand it in relation to culture. The doctrinal and the moral are simply inseparable because what we believe to be true is but the flip side of how we believe we should act, and vice versa. This is not to say that people with differing beliefs cannot agree upon a common course of action—that is, where there are doctrinal divisions, people might still unite in common service. But it is to say that the accounts people give of the significance of their actions might vary widely, and may indeed be incommensurable, such that there is no real agreement in action without an agreement in conviction, at least not if we are to speak of a *moral* act.

Second, in light of the unity of knowing and doing, ecumenical dialogue and consensus seems a more daunting venture than we might have imagined in the past. This is true whether one prioritizes knowing or doing. If we take seriously the analogy of belief systems with ecosystems, then there is a real sense in which one cannot address a piece without addressing the whole. Have we reached consensus on justification if we continue to differ on what constitutes social justice? Can there be real agreement in theological anthropology so long as differences remain over the practice of marriage? Piecemeal agreements on specific doctrines, as well as piecemeal alliances made around specific moral issues, do not necessarily fit together to form a larger whole that we might call "Christian unity." They may, in fact, constitute nothing more than a heap of fragments that the slightest wind could blow apart.

Finally, and maybe more hopefully, as daunting as the task is, we might still believe that the ecumenical venture, even the venture to reach agreement on contentious moral issues, is not impossible. True, it is taken up piecemeal—now this doctrine, now that moral question—but this is true of everything in life. We live in a world in which knowing and doing are always going on at the same time, but we find our way through that world in a piecemeal fashion. So there is no in-principle objection to taking up issues as they come and reaching consensus as best we can, as long as we recognize that such consensus will be provisional and that it may have to be revisited in light of a later issue that comes up for discussion. We must be open to the possibility that the agreement that we thought we had regarding theological anthropology might prove to be of insufficient depth when we come to discuss the practices of marriage. Likewise, we ought not to be surprised if our agreement on a matter of social justice begins to unravel once we examine the differing beliefs that undergird our practices. But just because the venture proves to be more complex than we imagined does not mean that it is impossible. Indeed, Christ's prayer for the unity of the Church ought to compel us to believe that it is possible.

4

Internal Injuries:
Moral Division within the Churches

Joseph D. Small

As God's chosen ones, holy and beloved, clothe yourselves with compassion, kindness, lowliness, meekness, and patience. Bear with one another and, if anyone has a complaint against another, forgive each other; just as the Lord has forgiven you, so you also must forgive. Above all, clothe yourselves with love, which binds everything together in perfect harmony. And let the peace of Christ rule in your hearts, to which indeed you were called in the one body.

—COLOSSIANS 3:12–15

In general the churches . . . bore for me the same relation to God that billboards did to Coca-Cola: they promoted thirst without quenching it.

—JOHN UPDIKE, *A MONTH OF SUNDAYS*

IT IS AN INSIDIOUS paradox of Reformed churches that our theological commitment to the unity of the church is paired with the reality of our continual schisms. Reformed churches have been central to the quest for the unity of Christ's church, but at the same time they have been internally injured by constant division and subdivision. Of the great ecclesial movements emerging from the sixteenth-century Reformation and its aftermath, it is the Reformed family of churches that has multiplied by a continual process of division born of disagreement, controversy, and partition. In the United States alone there are twenty-seven Reformed denominations, and this does not number churches with forgotten Reformed roots—Baptists and churches of the Stone-Campbell movement. Korea, the pride of Presbyterian missionaries, is now home to ninety-two Presbyterian denominations, and counting!

At the outset, the restored unity of the church was understood to be reformation's goal. John Calvin's critique of the late medieval Catholic Church and its practices was pervasive and often harsh, yet its purpose was always reform, not separation. More than two decades after Luther's dramatic challenge to Rome, a young Calvin wrote an open letter to Cardinal Sadoleto in which he acknowledged that the most serious of Catholic charges against the reformers was "that we have attempted to dismember the Spouse of Christ. Were that true," he continued, "both you and the whole world might regard us as desperate." While acknowledging the reality of division within the church, Calvin maintained that the reformers "desired nothing more than that religion being revived, the Churches, which discord had scattered and dispersed, might be gathered together into true unity."[1]

As the years passed, Calvin became increasingly disturbed by the fragmentation of the church. As the Council of Trent was concluding its sixteenth session, he wrote to Archbishop of Canterbury Thomas Cranmer, agonizing, "This other thing also is to be ranked among the chief evils of our time, viz., that the Churches are so divided, that human fellowship is scarcely now in any repute among us. . . . Thus it is that the members of the Church being severed, the body lies bleeding."[2] As late as 1560, while Trent was still in session, he wrote to the persecuted Reformed churches in France concerning his conviction that a universal council of the church was necessary to put an end to the divisions in Christendom. The hoped-for council should include representatives from the whole church, Calvin wrote, for he assumed inclusion of the Catholic bishops in the council together with

---

1. "Calvin's Reply to Sadoleto," in *A Reformation Debate: Sadoleto's Letter to the Genevans and Calvin's Reply*, ed. John C. Olin (New York: Fordham University Press, 2000) 87.

2. Calvin, "Letter to Cranmer" (1552), in *Selected Works of John Calvin: Tracts and Letters*, ed. Henry Beveridge and Jules Bonnet (Grand Rapids: Baker, 1983) 5:355

elected persons who desired the reform of the church. He was even open to the possibility that the pope would preside (but not rule) over the council.[3]

Of course, Calvin's hopes were not realized. Within a generation the Protestant movement had split into distinct branches—Lutheran, Reformed, Anabaptist, and Anglican—that became increasingly distant from, and often hostile to, one another. In turn, these branches splintered along national and theological lines, so that, in our time, thousands of separate churches are strewn across the world. Church divisions are occasionally healed, but most have endured, so that denominationalism is simply "the way things are" for most contemporary Christians. Among Protestants, division is assumed to be the normal condition of the church, and when disputes arise, subdivision is too often the first impulse rather than the last resort.

Sixteenth- and seventeenth-century divisions were largely theological, and most contemporary ecumenical dialogues address those continuing theological differences in a search for convergence, consensus, and agreement. But deep disagreements over moral issues have also been present from the beginning. In the United States, many churches coped with tensions over moral issues ranging from temperance to slavery, with some leading to threats of separation and the reality of division. Presbyterian schism over the issue of slavery predated the Civil War, and the north-south split endured until 1982!

In our time, deep disagreement over moral issues has come to dominate the lives of many churches. Actual schism has now occurred in the Episcopal Church and the Presbyterian Church (USA), while the Evangelical Lutheran Church faces that prospect this summer. Tragic fissures in the Anglican Communion threaten to disengage provinces, reducing some of them to mere national denominations. In all of these divisions, the place of gay and lesbian persons in the church is the defining moral issue, and although it is played out in slightly different ways in various churches, the disputes are centered on ordained ministry, and recently on "same-sex marriage" as well. It is not immaterial to the conflicts that ordained ministry is central, for in spite of our talk about its servant character, it is what provides access to power in the institutional life of the churches.

---

3. Calvin, "Letter to the Reformed Churches of France" (1560), in ibid., 7:168–70.

The Broadening Church

Mainline American Protestant churches long ago determined that significant theological latitude was tolerable. Presbyterians abandoned strict subscription to the Westminster Confession in the early eighteenth century, requiring only that ministers adopt the confession's "essential tenets," which, intentionally, were not identified. Today, my church asks ordinands to vow only that they will be "led, guided, and instructed" by the ten creeds, confessions, and catechisms in *The Book of Confessions*. The abandonment of rigid confessional subscription, as welcome as it was necessary, led to a progressive broadening of the range of acceptable theological perspectives. Theological diversity is now considered desirable; the constitution of the Presbyterian Church (USA) concludes its chapter on the unity of the church with a section on "Diversity and Inclusiveness" that includes "different theological positions" in its long list of required representational categories.[4]

In the wake of nearly three decades of divisive debates about the ordination of gay and lesbian persons, the PCUSA General Assembly commissioned a Theological Task Force on the Peace, Unity, and Purity of the Church. Its charge was to deal with evident unrest in the church around Christology, biblical authority and interpretation, ordination standards, and power. The 2006 report of the task force was admirable in many respects, yet it failed to settle any of the unrest. Its sections on Christology and the Bible were unremarkable, setting forth broad generalities as indications of widespread agreement in the church. Its work on ordination standards focused on the possibility of ordaining gay, lesbian, bisexual, and transgender persons, and so only led to another round of political battles. And, tellingly, the task force neglected to deal with power at all. Because theological diversity was assumed to be the desirable norm within the agreed upon generalities, the task force report failed to address deeper theological difficulties in the church, of which disputes about Christology, Scripture, ordination, and power are only symptoms.

Theological broadening of the Presbyterian Church has deep roots. The fundamentalist-modernist controversy of the early decades of the twentieth century was played out forcefully in the Presbyterian Church. The result was that attempts to enumerate essential theological tenets were

4. Presbyterian Church (USA), *Book of Order* (Louisville: Office of the General Assembly, 2009) G-4.0403

pushed to the background while essential social tenets were given pride of place. The 1910 General Assembly provided insight into what was to come. The Assembly adopted a list of five essential theological tenets, mere rewordings of the five Niagara fundamentals—inerrant Scripture, virgin birth, substitutionary atonement, bodily resurrection, and Jesus' miracles. The Assembly also adopted a version of the Federal Council of Churches' "Social Creed of the Churches," listing fourteen social pronouncements ranging from the equitable distribution of wealth, to reform of labor laws, to women's rights, to prison reform.[5] While the five theological fundamentals were soon abandoned, the causes of the social creed were incorporated into the church's institutional structures, budgets, and programs.

The fate of the essential tenets and the social creed was captured in the motto "theology divides, service unites." But it was not to be. Brad Longfield notes that "the path the church finally took in an effort to maintain its witness to the world probably only served to undermine that witness. . . . Without clear theological boundaries, the church, in the years ahead, would find it more and more difficult to maintain an identity separate from the culture and offer a unique message and vision to the world it sought to serve."[6] The severing of theology from morality was just one instance of the American churches' separation of (private) faith from (public) life. Belief was consigned to the province of the individual while the church went about the business of shaping ecclesial life and working to shape American society. Inevitably, then, "service"—mission, ethics, morality—came to be the flashpoint of disagreement and discord while thin agreement on theological platitudes provided weak bonds of institutional communion.

A decade ago, David Yeago characterized denominations as "institutional vessels designed to enclose extreme religious plurality." In denominations where "diversity" is the order of the day, he wrote, "Every party within the church is thus reduced to a *club*, boosters of a favorite style or commodity, and therefore to a phenomenon that mainline denominations are equipped to manage."[7] Yeago was writing about diverse interpreta-

---

5. For the texts of the two actions, see Maurice W. Armstrong, Lefferts A. Loetscher, and Charles A. Anderson, eds., *The Presbyterian Enterprise: Sources of American Presbyterian History* (Eugene, OR: Wipf & Stock, 2001) 278–82.

6. Bradley J. Longfield, *The Presbyterian Controversy* (New York: Oxford University Press, 1991) 230.

7. David Yeago, "The Spirit, the Church, and the Scriptures: Biblical Inspiration and Interpretation Revisited," in *Knowing the Triune God: The Work of the Spirit in the Practices of the Church*, ed. James J. Buckley and David S. Yeago (Grand Rapids: Eerdmans, 2001) 78.

tions of Scripture, but his point had wider implications. Yet the capacity of denominations to manage diversity is breaking down in precisely those areas—ethics and mission—that were thought to unite by providing a large umbrella under which a variety of churchly activities could be carried out. Mission divides because it requires us to make public choices about moral issues. Denominational mission divides because its requirement of public choice about moral issues is detached from shared commitment to the depth of the apostolic faith.

Church Votes

We see moral issues as real and potential church-dividing issues throughout Scripture and in the life of the early church. In the first four centuries, conversion was not only a matter of changed belief but also of changed patterns of behavior and belonging. Catechumens may have struggled less to believe what Christians believed than to live as Christians taught. So it should not surprise us that moral issues are contentious and may become church-dividing. The gospel is not about what we think, but how we live. Both Old and New Testaments impel us toward determinations of how we are to live before the living God. There is no distinction between *kerygma* and *didache*, between *theologia* and *paraenesis*. The animating thrust of Scripture is to display how faith acts, urging us to lead a life worthy of the calling to which we have been called (Eph 4:1).

What should surprise us, or perhaps appall us, is the way the churches deal with the moral disagreements that dominate ecclesial life. Alasdair MacIntyre gives voice to what we know all too well about North American society:

> The most striking feature of contemporary moral utterance is that so much of it is used to express disagreements; and the most striking feature of the debates in which these disagreements are expressed is their interminable character. I do not mean by this just that such debates go on and on and on—although they do—but also that they apparently can find no terminus. There seems to be no rational way of securing moral agreement in our culture.[8]

Or in our churches. And perhaps there is no moral agreement in our churches because churchly moral utterance is too often little more than a vaguely

8. Alasdair MacIntyre, *After Virtue: A Study in Moral Theory*, 2nd ed. (Notre Dame: University of Notre Dame Press, 1984) 6.

religious version of society's conversation. Americans remain divided on the place of gay and lesbian persons in society, abortion, affirmative action, immigration issues, access to health care, and a host of issues that are as moral as they are political. Church debates, especially in national church assemblies, merely place a religious patina on generalized social categories of rights, hospitality, inclusion, and justice—or authority, responsibilities, cohesion, and righteousness. In general, the most accurate indicator of the direction in which the church will move is the direction in which society is moving. And society's trajectory on issues of homosexuality was settled when *Will and Grace* became a top ten TV show. (Incidentally, the names Will and Grace were no accident.)

But moral issues continue to trouble the churches. Because seemingly interminable church debates contribute to denominational disaffection and mainline decline, denominations have come to rely on a time-honored way of providing the needed terminus: *voting*. Denominations, acting as good democratic institutions, give to representative church assemblies the responsibility of voting on legislative proposals designed to end debates on contested moral issues by enacting one side of the argument into church policy and ecclesiastical law. "One side" of the reductionist "two sides" is enacted because democratic voting procedures always reduce an issue to yes or no, up or down, in or out.

C. P. Snow observed that "the number 2 is a very dangerous number . . . Attempts to divide anything into two ought to be regarded with much suspicion."[9] We in the church don't have to be told, for we are painfully aware of the dangers of dividing into two. The divisive issues of the past decades have been made intractable by their reduction to two opposing positions—positions on which we are expected to vote. Even our best-intentioned discussions reinforce polar divisions by guaranteeing a voice to "both sides of the issue"—as if any issue worth discussing has only two sides. Our commitment to democratic polities presses us toward legislative dualisms on every matter: reductionist dualisms reduced to stark choice.

To make matters worse, having been reduced to two sides, issues are further diminished by means of slogans, most often "rights" and "justice" at one pole, and "biblical authority" and "morality" at the other. All complexity and nuance is lost as church assemblies vote up or down on "justice" or "the

---

9. C. P. Snow, *The Two Cultures and a Second Look*, 2nd ed. (Cambridge: The University Press, 1964) 9.

Bible" without, of course, ever asking, *Whose Justice? Which Rationality?*[10] or *Whose Community? Which Interpretation?*[11] Church assemblies do not ask because they have been called into session to do business, not theology. Moreover, they are gatherings of strangers. The PCUSA General Assembly that will soon meet will consist of over seven hundred commissioners, half of them ministers and half elders, 90 percent of whom have never been to a General Assembly. They will vote on hundreds of proposals, only a fraction of which they have studied, and then return home with no continuing responsibility for the actions they have taken.

The churches actually imagine that general assemblies, churchwide assemblies, and general conventions can decide complex moral issues by voting in a bipolar framework. Voting produces winners and losers, of course, but it can work reasonably well in political arenas where winning and losing is the assumed outcome, even the name of the game. Voting works best, however, in situations where differences are encompassed within broad consensus regarding aims, so that balloting is about the best means to achieve those aims. Voting does not work well in situations of intractable polarity (witness the US Senate) or when fundamental issues of faith and life are at stake. What have votes produced besides narrow victories for one side or the other? The aftermath of voting is the absence of reception, and an ecclesial landscape littered with more legislative maneuvers, invocation of parliamentary rules, judicial appeals, trials in church courts, and the departure of ministers, congregations, and whole judicatories. All of this is followed by fierce, unseemly battles over property in civil courts.

An odd feature of the churches' hyper-democratic method of decision-making is that they act in virtual isolation from one another. Even churches in so-called full communion continue to vote on theological statements, moral positions, ordered ministries, and more without consultation, let alone the concurrence of their sister churches. The Groupe des Dombes' latest document, *"One Teacher": Doctrinal Authority in the Church*, notes that the churches cannot simply adopt every form of democratic debate. In addressing both Catholics and the churches of the Reformation, *"One Teacher"* asks "that all churches agree to share in the debate regarding problems of faith and morals which are raised in a new way, acting together to take decisions in common whenever possible, and accepting the gospel

10. Alasdair MacIntyre, *Whose Justice? Which Rationality?* (Notre Dame: University of Notre Dame Press, 1988).

11. Merold Westphal, *Whose Community? Which Interpretation?* (Grand Rapids: Baker Academic, 2009).

principle of mutual correction."[12] When the same moral issue faces the churches, it is a denial of their expressed desire for unity in Christ that they act as independent moral agents.

There are no easy answers to the question of how decision-making beyond the forced choice majority voting might occur in the church, but I am struck by a brief account in Stanley Hauerwas's wonderful memoir, *Hannah's Child*. While at Notre Dame, Hauerwas was a member of a Methodist church whose pastor wanted to move the congregation to weekly celebration of the Eucharist. After considerable study, the church board discussed the matter. The board seemed to be on board, so Hauerwas moved that it be put to a vote. The pastor, who had been quiet up till then, suddenly declared, "You will not vote on this issue." Hauerwas was startled; wasn't this just what the pastor had worked for? But the pastor reminded the board that the Eucharist is about the unity of the church. If the celebration of the Eucharist were determined by a majority vote, unity would be betrayed. Anyone in the congregation who had reservations needed to be heard first, and if there was strong dissent, the church would have to wait.[13]

I am less impressed by the details of the story than by its spirit. All too often, when a majority vote determines the matter, the unity of the church is betrayed. Presbyterian votes on contended moral issues often fall within the 52 percent to 48 percent range. Can it be said that the *church* has decided anything when half of the church dissents? The solution does not lie in so-called consensus methods of decision-making or in super majorities, for these only perpetuate the notion that legislation is the appropriate means of settling matters of faith and morals in the church. Decisions to change or not to change significant elements of the church's faith and life take time (an un-American concept).

The story of the Presbyterian Church's decision to ordain women to ministry is instructive. Presbyterians have a threefold ordained ministry: deacons, elders, and ministers of the Word and Sacrament. The church authorized the ordination of women as deacons in 1910, as elders in 1930, and as ministers in 1956. The decision to ordain women as ministers was taken after years of study and discussion, and although it was not without opposition, it was approved overwhelmingly by the General Assembly and,

12. Le Groupe des Dombes, *"One Teacher": Doctrinal Authority in the Church* (Grand Rapids: Eerdmans, 2010) 143.

13. Stanley Hauerwas, *Hannah's Child: A Theologian's Memoir* (Grand Rapids: Eerdmans, 2010) 141.

more important, received the required ratification from the presbyteries by a vote of 205-35. Women's ordination did not become a divisive issue until the 1970s when the church ruled that a man who could not participate in the ordination of a woman could not himself be ordained.

When it meets next month, the PCUSA's 219th General Assembly (2010) will have before it an overture from the Presbytery of Miami Valley that calls the church to acknowledge that there is no unity of conscience regarding ordination standards in the church, and further calls the church to refrain from legislative efforts to resolve the controversy. The overture calls for the church to "fast" from legislation, and to seek instead the mind of Christ over a period of years. The spirit of the proposal is faithful, but while it may be on the right track, it probably comes too late and is almost certainly doomed to defeat. What then is to be done?

Withdrawal?

Presbyterians have experienced formal schism at least three times in the twentieth century: the Orthodox Presbyterian Church in the 1930s, the Presbyterian Church in America in the 1960s and 1970s, and the Evangelical Presbyterian Church in the 1980s. Schism occurs when one part of the church goes its own way without regard for the whole. But what happens when the part that goes its own way without regard for the whole is the part that is in charge? Schism is not the only possibility. David Yeago contends that as a result of actions taken by last year's Churchwide Assembly, the ELCA is now in a state of "impaired communion"—not abolished communion, but communion that is nevertheless diminished, weakened, and damaged. "The question before us as a denomination," he writes, "is whether it is possible to endure this impairment without breaking communion altogether, either by public splits or by large numbers of congregations . . . going practically into a kind of 'internal exile.'"[14]

Since 2005, more than seventy congregations have left the PCUSA to become part of the Evangelical Presbyterian Church. Many more congregations are waiting to see what happens at next month's General Assembly. Still other congregations have "defected in place," not withdrawing but not sharing actively in the life of the whole church. I can only speak knowledgably about my own church, but "impaired communion" has characterized its life

14. David Yeago, "Facing Reality in the ELCA," February 6, 2010. Online: http://lutheranspersisting.wordpress.com/david-yeago-facing-reality-in-the-elca/.

for decades. Our impaired communion is less the loss of formal structures of communion than the emptying of those structures, draining them of relationships of mutual responsibility for one another and accountability to one another for the shape of our faith and life. Our internal injuries have gone untreated for too long, and so infection spreads throughout the body. Are the only options, then, schism, internal exile, or defection in place?

How should those who are angry or threatened or grieving or dismayed by the condition of the churches respond? Withdrawal in any form is an odd response from those who believe their own convictions to be consistent with historic Christian faith and life. Withdrawal may even be a faithless response from those who are charged to "preach the word, be urgent in season and out of season, convince, rebuke, and exhort, be unfailing in patience and in teaching" (2 Tim 4:2). There is no refuge in a popularized invisible/visible church distinction, as if withdrawal from the actual church is justified by the unity of all Christians in the invisible church. Platonic notions of an ideal church that no one can see, accompanied by abandonment of the pale shadow of church that we can see, have no place in Scripture. Calvin noted that Scripture sometimes speaks of "church" as that which is actually in God's presence and sometimes as all those we see who now profess Christ. But he goes on to say, "Just as we must believe, therefore, that the former church, invisible to us, is visible to the eyes of God alone, so we are commanded to revere and keep communion with the latter."[15] Communion with the actual church, with quite visible people and communities, cannot be dismissed as inconsequential, because we are "all one in Christ."

The Power of the Powerless

The question is pointed: How can Christians live with integrity in a church that they believe lacks a clear sense of what it means to live faithfully, as redeemed people, before God, as well as resolve to engage in a continuous, deep exploration of the faith? I suppose I should turn to Scripture at this point, but I have found some insight from an unexpected source: Václav Havel, playwright, essayist, dissident, resister, prisoner, and then, improbably, last president of Czechoslovakia and first president of the Czech Republic.

---

15. John Calvin, *Institutes of the Christian Religion*, trans. Ford Lewis Battles, ed. John T. McNeill (Philadelphia: Westminster, 1960) 4.1.7 (Battles, 1022).

Havel endured for decades under a repressive regime that lived within a lie and expected every citizen to live within the same lie. Havel and others struggled with a question that had daily consequences: how does one live freely within a system that suppresses freedom? For Havel, the answer lies in the difference between acceding to life within the lie and determining to live within the truth. His 1975 essay "The Power of the Powerless" is remarkable for the clarity of its vision, focusing on the strength of those who find themselves in opposition to prevailing social and political structures. What is the character of the established system, and what is the shape of resistance?

"Living within the lie can constitute the system only if it is universal," wrote Havel. "The principle must embrace and permeate everything. There are no terms whatsoever on which it can coexist with living within the truth, and therefore everyone who steps out of line *denies it in principle and threatens it in its entirety*."[16] Havel understands that in order for the lie to have power, it must be so commonly acknowledged that it is simply the way things are. But if some refuse to acknowledge the lie, if some confront the lie with truth, the lie cannot be established as customary reality. Havel illustrates his conviction by imagining a simple greengrocer who regularly follows the instructions of the state by displaying in his shop window a poster announcing the Marxist slogan, "Workers of the world, unite!" The grocer does not think about his action; he simply goes along with a seemingly trivial expression of the way things are in order to get along in a society that expects acquiescence.

Havel asks us to imagine that one day something in the greengrocer changes and he stops displaying the required slogan that he had imagined would ingratiate him to the system. He then carries his minor resistance further by ceasing to vote in the state's show elections and by expressing himself honestly at authorized political meetings. He even finds the strength to risk solidarity with other resisters. "In this revolt the greengrocer steps out of living within the lie. He rejects the ritual and breaks the rules of the game. . . . His revolt is an attempt to *live within the truth*."[17] What is the significance of the small act of an ordinary greengrocer, especially in light of the fact that his defiance will not go unpunished? Havel simply notes that "as long as appearance is not confronted with reality, it does not seem to be

16. Václav Havel, "The Power of the Powerless," in *Václav Havel: Living in Truth*, ed. Jan Vladislav (London: Faber & Faber, 1986) 56. Italics in original.

17. Ibid., 55.

appearance. As long as living a lie is not confronted with living the truth, the perspective needed to expose its mendacity is lacking. As soon as the alternative appears, however, it threatens the very existence of appearance and living a lie . . ."[18]

Before going further with Václav Havel, we must acknowledge that the Presbyterian, Lutheran, Episcopal, and other churches are not totalitarian regimes. Their lives are not characterized by comprehensive "living within the lie," and their ecclesial systems do not suppress dissent. Soviet-dominated Czechoslovakia is not an analog to mainline churches, and the current situation within the churches does not correspond to the plight of dissenting citizens confronted by the real and present danger of harsh repression and punishment. Nevertheless, with these necessary disclaimers having been made and with necessary shifts in perspective having been made possible, Havel's analysis and strategies provide insights that are relevant to the current ecclesial situation in American Christianity.

Our churches are characterized by illusions about the character of their (diverse) faith, illusions about their assertions of (democratic) power, and illusions about the premium they place on expressions of (institutional) harmony. These misapprehensions are not limited to matters of morality. They are pervasive throughout the life of the church. Our churches deceive themselves by making a virtue of wildly diverse theological positions on basic Christian belief, by imagining that the mechanisms of parliamentary procedure ensure faithful determination of faith and practice, and by equating cheerful or grudging acquiescence with genuine unity. Ecclesial self-deceit finds expression in the naïve expectation that all within the church will celebrate diversity, treasure the processes of governance, and happily support the current state of the church's faith and life (all, of course, in the name of "mission").

So, while our situation is not the same as Havel's, and our question is not the same as Havel's, his question informs our own. Our question is how we can live *with integrity* in churches if we believe they lack a clear sense of the faith, and thus lack a clear sense of what it means to live faithfully, as redeemed people, before God.

Havel's greengrocer is a simple illustration of the refusal to live within the lie, but the greengrocer alone does not present an exemplary strategy. In order for the greengrocer's refusal to be other than quixotic, he must first be joined to other "greengrocers." Havel understands that "living within

---

18. Ibid., 56.

the truth covers a vast territory whose outer limits are vague and difficult to map, a territory full of modest expressions of human volition, the vast majority of which will remain anonymous and whose political impact will probably never be felt."[19] One trusts that many pastors will preach and teach truthfully, many elders will labor to ensure congregational fidelity, many deacons will lead in ministries of compassion and justice, and many members will pray, study, and serve. But while individual living—and individual congregational living—in greater integrity is necessary, it is not adequate to the apostolic call to use the gifts we have been given "for building up the body of Christ, until we all attain to the unity of the faith and of the knowledge of the Son of God" (Eph 4:12–13).

Havel takes us beyond the greengrocer: "The point where living within the truth ceases to be a mere negation of living with a lie and becomes articulate in a particular way, is the point at which something is born that might be called 'the independent spiritual, social, and political life of society.'"[20] For Havel, the "independent life of society" is a communal environment in which living within the truth becomes articulate and apparent. Public dissent and formal opposition may emerge, but "the original and most important sphere of activity, one that predetermines all the others, is simply an attempt to create and support the 'independent life of society' as an articulated expression of 'living within the truth.' In other words, serving truth consistently, purposefully and articulately, and organizing this service."[21] Living within the truth is a *social* reality, not merely an individual stance.

What would it mean, within our churches, to *serve truth consistently, purposefully and articulately,* and equally important, to *organize this service*? Negation—opposing or seeking to reverse some recent actions of church assemblies—may well be necessary, but it is only a minor part of serving truth. Consistent, purposeful, and articulate serving of the truth entails renewed determination to proclaim and teach the faith in worship, in groups, in sessions, vestries, and councils, in congregations, in dioceses and presbyteries, in national expressions of the church, through spoken words, publications and other media, and consistent action. The church's expression of Havel's *independent life of society* that lives within the truth

19. "Power of the Powerless," 85.

20. Ibid.

21. Ibid., 87.

requires more than the effort of individual pastors and congregations; it requires *organizing this service.*

Organizing this service entails the creation of a different culture within the church. "When those who have decided to live within the truth," says Havel, "begin to create what I have called the independent life of society, this independent life begins, of itself, to become structured in a certain way."[22] What is this structuring like? Havel begins with a term borrowed from nonconformist music and art—"second culture." For him, second culture refers to a broad-ranging expression of independent and suppressed culture in the humanities, social sciences, and philosophical thought, as well as the arts. The second culture is a way of being that does not accede to the way things are. It resists prevailing patterns and expressions by creating new arrangements and articulations. A second culture resists the predominant culture by way of innovation rather than negation.

At this time, a second culture within the church could be built by those who understand that the most important task is creating space within which a new community of persons can engage in thinking the faith, preaching and teaching the faith, praying the faith, and living the faith. This culture will require that many "greengrocers" attend to the faith as a calling that is higher than managerial effort, programmatic accomplishment, or congregational success. It is a culture characterized by pastors who become "teachers of the faith" in more than name; congregational governance that spends more time in study and discernment of the spiritual welfare of the congregation than in fiduciary management; deacons who live out biblical ministries of compassion and justice; and members who worship, study, serve, and share faithfulness. This culture also requires substantial patterns of mutual affirmation (and admonition) that support the sustained effort of many.

Second cultures are dynamic, pressing toward new expressions that raise "organizing this service" to more intense levels of engagement. "Second cultures," the milieu of independent thought and expression, are where what Havel calls "parallel structures" emerge. Parallel structures are not simply duplicate ecclesiastical institutions, much less separated churches. They are, according to Havel, "an area where a different life can be lived, a life that is in harmony with its own aims and which in turn structures itself

---

22. "Power of the Powerless," 100f.

in harmony with those aims."[23] Parallel structures give recognizable, shared form to the second culture.

The institutions of prevailing ecclesial systems must be met by parallel structural possibilities. The creation of parallel structures should not be confused with the creation of shadow institutions. In recent years, Presbyterian institutions have not served us well. Creating mirror images of those institutions in the hope that organizational/managerial approaches to Christian faith and life can be done better and more faithfully misses an opportunity to embody a new way of living the gospel. Within the church, genuinely parallel structures might include intentional networks, collaborative educational efforts, covenanted spiritual disciplines of Scripture and prayer, alternative ecumenical relations, focused mission initiatives, and more. Parallel structural possibilities may also include judicatory realignments and even the creation of non-geographic presbyteries, synods, and dioceses. But method is not the point. Whatever the shape of parallel structures, they will only be worthwhile if they *live* differently from current church institutions, avoiding the bourgeois values and bureaucratic procedures that too often characterize church life.

The essential point is that *concrete possibilities* with discernable *structural form* must emerge from *alternative culture* lest *integrity* be little more than private righteousness. Parallel structures are the most articulate expressions of living within the truth, for parallel structures necessarily imply a parallel *polis*, that is, a *community* that thinks, talks, and acts in mutuality. Václav Havel insists that "it would be quite wrong to understand the parallel structures . . . as a retreat into a ghetto and as an act of isolation, addressing itself only to those who had decided on such a course, and who are indifferent to the rest. It would be wrong, in short, to consider it an essentially group solution that has nothing to do with the general situation."[24] Havel's contention—one that should resonate with Christians who face ecclesial choices—is that withdrawal separates "living within the truth" from its proper point of departure, which is "concern for others." Withdrawal—whether formal or private—is "just another more sophisticated version of 'living within a lie.'"[25]

The responsibility of any person, congregation, second culture, and parallel structure within the church is responsibility for the whole church.

23. Ibid., 102.
24. Ibid., 103.
25. Ibid.

Havel understands what we in the church imperfectly grasp: "the parallel *polis* points beyond itself and only makes sense as an act of deepening one's responsibility to and for the whole, as a way of discovering the most appropriate *locus* for this responsibility, not as an escape from it."[26] A parallel *polis* within the church must not become a mode of distance from our denominations, but rather a deepening of responsibility for them by the living out of truthful witness within and for the whole church.

The task before those who desire to live within the truth is to create a "second culture," expressed in "parallel structures," as the shape of a "parallel *polis*." This means something different from loose alliances, programmatic organizations, missional associations, and focused mission groups, although it may include them. What is needed is a committed, organized, ecclesial *polis* that gives shape to discernable arrangements of mutual responsibility and accountability embodying enduring relationships of communion that summon the whole church into the joy of living within the truth. Only a parallel *polis* that emerges from an alternative culture shaped by renewed and deepened fidelity to the gospel will display the grace of the Lord Jesus Christ, the love of God, and the communion of the Holy Spirit.

The point of it all is not merely to think differently, but to live differently. The aim is not to critique the illusions of others, but to display an alternate way of performing the gospel. What all of this means concretely will only become clear as persons in the churches commit themselves to live within the truth by seeking to embody a "second culture" that nurtures "parallel structures" that build a "parallel *polis*"—all for the sake of the full gospel and the life of the whole church.

Do I expect something like this to happen? I cannot speak about other churches, but I do not expect it in my own church. At least I do not expect that it will emerge from the efforts of Presbyterian ministers, members, and congregations. Our internal injuries are now chronic disabilities. And yet perhaps the Spirit will create "greengrocers" among us.

Having begun with a John Updike novel, I close with one of Søren Kierkegaard's parables:

> When in a written examination the youth are allotted four hours to develop a theme, then it is neither here nor there if an individual student happens to finish before the time is up, or uses the entire time. Here, therefore, the task is one thing, the time another. But when the time itself is the task, it becomes a fault to finish before

26. Ibid., 104.

the time has transpired. Suppose a man were assigned the task of entertaining himself for an entire day, and he finishes this task of self-entertainment as early as noon: then his celerity would not be meritorious. So also when life constitutes the task. To be finished with life before life has finished with one, is precisely not to have finished the task.[27]

27. Søren Kierkegaard, *Concluding Unscientific Postscript*, in *Parables of Kierkegaard*, ed. Thomas C. Oden (Princeton: Princeton University Press, 1978) 85.

5

Unity in the Sacraments and Unity in Ethics

Susan K. Wood

A CORRELATION BETWEEN LITURGY and ethics dates back to the Old Testament. For instance, in the book of Amos, the Lord does not delight in solemn assemblies or accept burnt offerings and grain offerings in the absence of justice and righteousness (Amos 5:12). In the New Testament, Paul chastises the Corinthian community for their scandalous behavior at their gatherings for the Lord's Supper where each went ahead with his or her own supper and one goes hungry while another becomes drunk (1 Cor 11:20–21). What is the relationship, however, between ethical action and the liturgy? What is the relationship between the moral body and the liturgical body, between ethics and ecclesiology? The relationship between sacramental unity and unity in ethics depends on how the relationship between liturgy and ethics is conceived. I will identify a number of models that illustrate different relationships between liturgy and ethics and then determine the nature of the unity for each. The models are not necessarily incompatible with one another. Some are more superficial than others, but a combination of them can operate simultaneously. Some have more affinity with Protestant traditions, often espousing a theology of the word, while others have a greater correspondence with ecclesial traditions having more of a sacramental ontology.

Liturgy as Instrument of Ethics

In an instrumentalist view of the liturgy, liturgy is used as a tool in the development of ethical concepts and behaviors. Edward Philips cites Roman Catholic Masses for world peace or Protestant "litanies" for social justice as examples of such liturgy as a tool for ethics.[1] He also cites the use of liturgical song as a motivational tool. The danger of liturgical instrumentalism is that it often falls prey to moralism. It commodifies the liturgy for an external agenda. In its worst forms, it has the potential of manipulating the assembly for an extrinsic purpose, as if we worship only to become better people. This reverses the directionality of worship from being theocentric, directed to God, to being anthropocentric, directed toward the betterment of human life.

Liturgy as Exemplar of Ethics

When liturgy functions as an exemplar of ethics, both liturgy and ethics function mimetically. We are to imitate in life what we perform liturgically. An example here is the enactment of Jesus' washing the feet of the disciples during the Easter Vigil (John 13:1–16). Here the liturgy of the footwashing mimics the gospel narrative, and the ethical action of figuratively washing one another's feet in mutual service is mimetic of the liturgical action.

Liturgy as Formative of Moral Character

A number of both moral theologians and liturgists have developed correlations between liturgy and character ethics. For example, Stanley Hauerwas stresses the narrative aspect of liturgy as formative of Christian character.[2] For Hauerwas, "the sacraments enact the story of Jesus, and, thus, form

1. Edward Phillips, "Liturgy and Ethics," in *Liturgy in Dialogue: Essays in Memory of Ronald Jasper*, ed. Paul Bradshaw and Bryan Spinks (Collegeville, MN: Liturgical, 1995) 88–101, 96.

2. Stanley Hauerwas, *Character and the Christian Life: A Study in Theological Ethics* (San Antonio: Trinity University Press, 1975); *A Community of Character: Towards a Constructive Christian Social Ethic* (Notre Dame: University of Notre Dame Press, 1981); *The Peaceable Kingdom* (Notre Dame: University of Notre Dame Press, 1983). M. Therese Lysaught echoes this perspective in "Love and Liturgy," in *Gathered for the Journey: Moral Theology in Catholic Perspective*, ed. David Matzko McCarthy and M. Therese Lysaught (Grand Rapids: Eerdmans, 2007) 24–42, esp. 33–34.

a community in his image";[3] the sacraments shape and prepare us to tell and hear that story. In telling the story, we enter into it and become part of the story. In baptism, we enter into Christ's death and resurrection. In the Eucharist, we become part of Christ's sacrifice and enter into his kingdom.[4] This approach is also that of Richard Gula, an ethicist who has also written on the sacrament of reconciliation, as well as the liturgist Don Saliers.[5]

Broadly taken, Christian narrative as recounted either in the Scriptures or the liturgy provides the vision or particular view of life that is formative of Christian character. In narrative ethics, I become what I see. I am shaped by the narrative world into which I immerse myself. A master narrative runs through readings, songs, and images in the texts and rituals that circumscribe this world. This narrative forms the basis of character, which in turn leads to a specific ethical activity. This ethical activity is not only prescribed within the narratives but also arises from imitation of the values and ethos within the narrative. The narrative provides an interpretation of the world in its account of good and evil, the goal of authentic human living, and its embedded theology of God and God's will regarding human activity. The Christian story leads to a Christian worldview, which leads to Christian character, which leads to a Christian ethics. This interrelationship leads Saliers to remark, "as we worship so we shall be."[6] In addition to communicating the foundational and governing narrative of a community, ritual actions symbolically enact the root images and narratives by which a community understands itself to be living worthily. He distinguishes this from "mere *memesis*," understood as a simple "imitation of Christ," insofar as "such worship is best understood as a participation in the symbols of faith which is effected and signified by the words and actions of Christ."[7]

---

3. Hauerwas, *Peaceable Kingdom,* 107.

4. Ibid., 107–8.

5. Richard Gula, *Reason Informed by Faith: Foundations of Catholic Morality* (New York: Paulist, 1989); *To Walk Together Again: The Sacrament of Reconciliation* (New York: Paulist, 1984); Don E. Saliers, "Pastoral Liturgy and Character Ethics: As We Worship So We Shall Be," in *Source and Summit: Commemorating Josef A. Jungmann, SJ,* ed. Joanne M. Pierce and Michael Downey (Collegeville, MN: Liturgical, 1999) 183–194; "Liturgy and Ethics: Some New Beginnings," *Journal of Religious Ethics* 7:2 (1979) 173–89, and reiterated in ch. 13 of *Worship as Theology: Foretaste of Glory Divine* (Nashville: Abingdon, 1994). This essay was also republished in *Liturgy and the Moral Self: Humanity at Full Stretch Before God,* ed. Byron Anderson and Bruce T. Morrill (Collegeville, MN: Liturgical, 1998) 15–35.

6. This is the subtitle of his article "Pastoral Liturgy and Character Ethics," 183.

7. Saliers, "Liturgy and Ethics: Some New Beginnings," 180.

Character ethics represents an advance over a rule-based ethics because it is more comprehensive of the human person. It is an analysis based not just on human action, but encompasses the whole range of what it means to be human including motivations, affectivity, and intentionality. Moreover, character ethics is not just the ethics of an individual, but can characterize whole communities of discourse and practice. It emphasizes that which we as a community cherish most deeply and are willing to die for. The moral life of the community becomes the embodiment of those virtues, affections, and actions of Christ, whose paschal mystery we narrate biblically and celebrate liturgically. In the narrative and in the liturgy, we literally "put on Christ." Saliers, in correlating the formative power of the liturgy with character ethics, aptly demonstrates a convergence between the two disciplines insofar as each is concerned with formation by the Christian narrative. It is this narrative that is normative for ethical action, and both character ethics and liturgical worship are about shaping ethical actors by the language and symbols that convey that narrative. The presupposition is that Christian formation will lead to Christian behaviors.

Although not always recognized as such, character ethics is an extended theology of the word.[8] Even when rituals and sacramental symbols play a vital role in shaping a Christian worldview, they function as embodied words of that master narrative.

Liturgy Identified with Ethics

According to another view, liturgy *is* ethics; they are one and the same thing. For example, the ethicist John Howard Yoder argues, "liturgy and ethics are virtually identical ways in which the Christian community lives out the gospel."[9] For Yoder, "what the New Testament is talking about in 'breaking bread' is believers' actually sharing with one another their ordinary day-to-day material substance."[10] Bread does not symbolize values of hospitality and community, the values being somehow distinguishable from the signs

8. William W. Everett, in "Liturgy and Ethics: A Response to Saliers and Ramsey," *Journal of Religious Ethics* 7:2 (1979) 203–214, identifies both Saliers and Paul Ramsey as "disciples of theologies of the Word rather than of Pentecostal ecstasy or sacramental symbolics," 203.

9. John Howard Yoder, "Sacrament as Social Process: Christ the Transformer of Culture," *Theology Today* 48 (1991) 33–44.

10. Ibid., 37.

that refer to them. Instead, "bread *is* daily sustenance. Bread eaten together *is* economic sharing."[11] Meaning is not distinguishable from the act itself, nor the act from its meaning. Operationally, what we do in baptism and in "breaking bread" is ethics, is egalitarianism and economic ethics, respectively, before it is overlaid with any other sacramental meaning.

Weaknesses of Previous Models

These three approaches—liturgy as instrument of ethics, liturgy as exemplar of ethics, and liturgy as formative of moral character—suffer from a number of significant weaknesses. In the liturgy as instrument model, the danger is liturgical reductionism since only the (seemingly) ethically relevant texts and actions count.[12] This model runs the serious risk of politicizing the liturgy.

Margaret Farley rightly notes that a theology of liturgy as formative of character remains a formal principle with little translation in terms of the concrete pressing moral issues of our times.[13] Two millennia of corporate liturgical worship have not sufficiently formed a corporate conscience empowered to take a stand against evil and for good on the specific issues of the day—issues of welfare reform, corporate investment, women's rights, affirmative action, abortion, capital punishment, full employment, and disarmament, among others. Of this list, there are some Christian churches who have taken a stand on abortion, but not all. Some churches have taken official stances on war, siding for pacifism, or on capital punishment. Too often, however, moral issues become dividing for churches reading the same biblical narrative and practicing baptism and the Lord's Supper, some taking stances on the issues of individual sexual morality and others taking stands on war and social issues. Cardinal Bernadin's consistent ethic of life all too often continues to be a lone prophetic voice.[14] Formally, perhaps many Christian churches admit that all these are moral issues requiring moral action, but formal principles do not easily unite concrete practices.

---

11. Ibid.

12. Phillips, "Liturgy and Ethics," 100.

13. Margaret Farley, "Beyond the Formal Principle: A Reply to Ramsey and Saliers," *Journal of Religious Ethics* 7:2 (1979) 191–202.

14. Cardinal Joseph Bernadin, *Consistent Ethic of Life* (Kansas City: Sheed & Ward, 1988).

We have learned neither to form a corporate conscience nor to live with integrity the pluralism that makes the social ethics of the church today.

Character ethics functions within a defined community with a defined biblical text and a prescribed liturgy. Thus it is essentially an ethic for that community, an ethic for the church. Lisa Sowe Cahill critiques the communitarian ethic of Hauerwas for rejecting the liberal presupposition that there exists a universal ethics or universal ethical values.[15] This is in contradistinction to natural law ethics or the Catholic social teaching tradition, both of which purport to teach universal values and norms for such diverse issues as war and peace, economic justice, the rights and responsibilities of families and married couples, and biomedical issues such as in vitro fertilization. Cahill rehearses the criticisms of Hauerwas's project: claims of tribal sectarianism, of rendering ethics inaccessible to rational criteria of truth and validity, of the promotion of a dualist worldview, of not allowing for the need of purification of the church, and of not admitting a diversity of cultural voices and insights.[16]

Yet another criticism of character ethics is voiced by William W. Everett, who finds that in character ethics, "the weight of concern falls on the personal and psychological first, the institutional second."[17] He also finds that the models are more informed by the past narrative than by an altogether new eschatological vision. However, Everett would probably be as critical of any sacramental view of ethics as he is of character ethics since he finds both narrative and worship as falling into sectarianism and therefore not being effective in a pluralistic milieu.[18] He finds that they legitimize institutions, particularly the church, rather than orienting individuals toward "society."

The problem with Yoder's *identification of liturgy with ethics* is that it fails to distinguish between two modalities, the symbolic and the historical, and so effectively collapses both into the same plane of reality, the historical. This model eliminates the eschatological orientation of the liturgy as symbolizing what is not yet achieved historically at the same time that it deprives history of its *telos,* its directionality to final completion. It also evacuates the symbolic, rendering it literal.

---

15. Lisa Sowle Cahill, "L'Éthique communautarienne et le Catholicisme Américain," *Recherches de Sciences Religieuses* 95 (2007) 21–40, 29.

16. Ibid., 31.

17. Everett, "Liturgy and Ethics: A Response to Saliers and Ramsey," 203.

18. Ibid., 207.

Ethics as Verification of Liturgy: The Theology of Louis-Marie Chauvet

A more recent account of liturgy and ethics that potentially avoids the pitfalls mentioned above is that of the liturgist Louis-Marie Chauvet.[19] Chauvet is a sacramentalist for whom ethics is not merely an imitation of Jesus' ethical action or a living out of a worldview presented in the liturgy, but the means of giving God a body in the world; not merely the moral formation of subjects within worship, ethics itself constitutes worship in the world. It is distinct from both word and sacrament, but is also a different modality of expressing the same reality narrated in word and symbolically embodied in sacrament. Chauvet's ethics differs from sectarian ethics in that worship is not sacralization, that is, a setting apart from the profane, but is the sanctification of the profane. Liturgy does not verify ethics, but ethics verifies the liturgy. This means that ritual offering is not sufficient in itself. As Chauvet expresses it, "The *ritual* dispossession in honor of God is meaningful only if it is 'veri-fied' (made genuine) in an *existential* dispossession in favor of those in need."[20] In Chauvet's thought, "the rite is the *symbolic expression* of an ethical duty," and "grace is always given as a tasked to be performed."[21] In other words, the prime location of worship is "the ethics of everyday life sanctified by theological faith and charity."[22] This reversal of sacralization does not create an ethics that is different from that of Jews, Muslims, or others. The difference is not moral, the specific content of ethics, but theological. The theological faith of Christians indicates what

---

19. Louis-Marie Chauvet, *Symbol and Sacrament* (Collegeville, MN: Liturgical, 1995), English translation of *Symbole et Sacrament: Un relecture sacramentelle de l'existence chrétienne* (Paris: Cerf, 1987). Citations will reference the English edition. See also Chauvet, *The Sacraments: The Word of God at the Mercy of the Body* (Collegeville, MN: Liturgical, 2001). Secondary literature developing the connection between ethics and liturgy and Chauvet's thought includes Timothy M. Brunk, *Liturgy and Life: The Unity of Sacrament and Ethics in the Theology of Louis-Marie Chauvet* (New York: Peter Lang, 2007); Philippe Bordeyne, "The Ethical Horizon of Liturgy," and Bruce T. Morrill, "Time, Absence, and Otherness: Divine-Human Paradoxes Bonding Liturgy and Ethics," in *Sacraments: Revelation of the Humanity of God,* ed. Philippe Bordeyne and Bruce T. Morrill (Collegeville, MN: Liturgical, 2008) 119–36 and 137–52.

20. Chauvet, *Sacraments,* 58.

21. Ibid.

22. Chauvet, *Symbol and Sacrament,* 262.

kind of critical relation is established in Christianity between religious and sacred manifestations and everyday ethical behavior.[23]

Chauvet's thought is richly complex. Here I will limit myself to tracing in broad strokes two passages or transitions that illustrate the interrelationships among Scripture, sacrament, and ethics in his thought. The first transition is from the book to the body, that is, from the narrative in the Scriptures to the social body of the people. Although Chauvet does not reference character ethics, this move seems similar to that model, since the community "writes itself into the Book" so that "the Book, in its very essence, seeks to permeate the whole volume of the social body of the people."[24] The task of discipleship is for the faithful to incorporate into themselves the Book of Scripture, rewritten as gospel, that is, the living good news of Jesus Christ. At this point, his thought appears similar to the formation by the liturgical worldview that is common to character ethics. However, for Chauvet, a reversal occurs, because in the "receptive listening" to God's law,[25] the social body does not just assume the text as its identity, but it recognizes itself, its living faith in the text proclaimed.[26] The community is not the exemplar of the text, but the text is the exemplar of the faith community, which first embodies the faith and then recognizes itself in the text. The community then writes itself into the book it reads such that the text becomes the community's autobiography.[27] The result is that "book and community are recognized as inseparable. The book is nothing without the community, and the community finds in the book the mirror of its identity. The norm is thus not the Book alone, but *the Book in the hand of the community*."[28] Here we move away from the principle of *sola scriptura*.[29] The book is thus transformed into the body because the body

23. Ibid.

24. Ibid., 263.

25. Ibid., 264.

26. Ibid., 208.

27. Chauvet does not use the term "autobiography," but George S. Worgul does when he comments on the challenge that ritual presents to the individual and community to interiorize or appropriate the foundational meaning of the community, stating that "ritual demands that role become autobiography." Worgul, "Ritual," in *The New Dictionary of Sacramental Worship*, ed. Peter E. Fink (Collegeville, MN: Liturgical, 1990) 1104. Within Chauvet's thought, the same would be true of the text read in the liturgy.

28. Ibid., 209. Italics in original.

29. This does not mean that Scripture ceases to norm the ethical life of the community, but that the gospel is also communicated within the life, worship, and teaching of

becomes its living referent, the living letter, the place of God's revelation, the place where God is manifested. This expresses Paul's sentiment when he writes, "You yourselves are our letter, written on our hearts, to be known and read by all; and you show that you are a letter of Christ, prepared by us, written not with ink but with the Spirit of the living God, not on tablets of stone but on tablets of human hearts" (2 Cor 3:2–3).[30] This first transition represents the transformation of the letter into the social body as well as a transition from Word to Church.

A second transition occurs from Church to ethics by way of sacrament. To develop this idea, Chauvet explores the symbolic nature of rituality. Noting that Westerners spontaneously tend to direct their attention to the ideas that the rite evokes, Chauvet insists that ritual is less mental than behavioral, functioning more at the level of the signifying than at the level of the signified and ideational content. Here we perhaps see another major difference between his thought and that of the character ethicists.

Chauvet applies a theory of symbolic exchange to the liturgy wherein he articulates the relationship between sacramental gratuity and ethical obligation. Every gift received obligates, but the gift given in return is never equivalent to the initial gift. Nor is it exterior to the person giving it, but, through an illocutionary dimension of language, "it is always ultimately oneself that one gives" in the given word.[31] The return-gift of the self is an ethical practice by which the subject verifies what he or she has received in the sacrament.[32] This exchange is of a completely different order from that of the marketplace or of value because of the incommensurability of the divine and human gifts.

Within the triad of "Scripture," "sacrament," and "ethics," "Scripture" corresponds to "gift," "sacrament" corresponds to "reception," and "ethics" corresponds to "return-gift."[33] Scripture is gift. It is a Christian reading of the Bible focused on the historical and glorious body of Christ, who is the gift of God, the "founding event," God's gift to us. This gift refers to a historical past that is not primarily our own history for which we are giving thanks, but a history that is radically other and past. This history is sacramentally recounted in the ritual anamnesis where we recognize this

---

the community. See *Dei Verbum*, 8, on the transmission of divine revelation.

30. Cited in Chauvet, *Symbol and Sacrament*, 264.

31. Ibid., 267.

32. Ibid., 281.

33. Ibid., 278–80.

apparently other history to be our own history. The time marker of this original gift is past insofar as it refers to a historical point in time when Jesus took on flesh.

Reception is identified sacramentally because "Jesus Christ, formerly given by God as a historical body raised up from the dead, is *today* received by us as *a sacramental body*, God's present."[34] This gift, however, is not a graspable object, but is only received and appropriated by the recipients "in dispossessing themselves of it through the oblation of giving thanks."[35] The time marker of the sacramental reception of the gift of Jesus Christ is present. The modality of sacramental reception is symbolic. The return-gift is specified as "Ethics" and "consists essentially in the agape between brothers and sisters."[36] The living-in-grace as brothers and sisters verifies, that is, makes genuine, the symbolic reception of the historical grace-bestowing God. This corresponds to the older tradition whereby the Church is the *corpus verum* ("real body") of Christ insofar as it is the *veritas* ("true reality") of his *corpus mysticum* ("his body in mystery," which is his sacramental body as understood until the middle of the twelfth century).[37] The time marker for the return-gift is future because it is only complete and completed eschatologically. The modality of this third stage, like the first stage, is historical, for the ethical appropriation of what is sacramentally and symbolically experienced in fullness in the present is lived out only chronologically and into the future. This ethical action is interpreted theologically and liturgically as a response to an initial gift of grace from God. This responsiveness is what makes such action a Christian ethics.

Chauvet identifies sacrament as a point of passage—no more, no less. This means that "it has neither its origin nor its end in itself." The point of departure is the gift from God in Jesus Christ. The point of arrival is what Chauvet calls the "missionary liturgy" of ethical practice.[38] The liturgy ends with the charge to go and do likewise—that is, to live out ethically, existentially, and historically what has just been celebrated sacramentally.

---

34. Ibid., 279.

35. Ibid.

36. Ibid.

37. Henri de Lubac traced the transposition of these terms from these meanings to the meaning more common today whereby the church is the *corpus mysticum* and the sacrament is the *corpus verum* in *Corpus Mysticum: L'Eucharistie et l'Eglise au Moyen Âge* (Paris: Aubier-Montagne, 1944).

38. Chauvet, *Symbol and Sacrament*, 281.

Chauvet is a sacramental theologian, not an ethicist. His synthesis of liturgy and ethics is incapable of specifying what constitutes specific ethical actions. His contribution is rather to show how the lived faith and action of a community relates to Scripture and sacrament as the lived embodiment of both.

Liturgy as Ethical Commitment

None of the above models speaks of liturgy as an ethical commitment. Liturgy does not just tell us what specific ethical activities to engage in, as liturgy as instrument does, nor shape our perception of an ethical Christian world, as liturgy as character ethics does, nor incorporate ethical actions into the liturgy, as liturgy as ethics does, nor sacramentally represent within symbolic time the ethical actions lived out in historical time. Liturgy speaks and accomplishes even more: it represents a moment of *kairos*, the decisive moment wherein a person assumes a new identity that establishes a new relationship with the world entailing ethical obligations. This is a sacramentalist rather than a strict narrative theology insofar as the liturgy effects a transformation within an individual.

Baptism, situated within the context of the Rite of Christian Initiation of Adults in the Catholic tradition, may be the most striking liturgical example of this model. Nonetheless, the Eucharist also entails ethical obligations and commitments to inclusive love, just distribution of resources, authority of service rather than domination, mutual self-sacrifice, and the like. Here I limit myself to illustrating the relationship between baptism and ethics.

The rite of initiation involves a spiritual journey of conversion that culminates in the reception of the sacraments of initiation: baptism, confirmation, and Eucharist. These initiate the catechumen into the faith community of the church at the same time that they conform the baptized to the pattern of Christ's death and resurrection and make him or her a member of the body of Christ. The time of preparation constitutes a state of liminality wherein the catechumen separates from his of her former life. Entrance into the catechumenate requires of the catechumens an initial conversion and an intention to change their lives. The rite enumerates the requirements as "evidence of the first stirrings of repentance, a start to the practice of calling upon God in prayer, a sense of the Church, and some experience of the company and spirit of Christians through contact with a priest or with members of the community."[39] During the period of the catechumenate, a series of exorcisms asking God to protect the catechumens from the spirit of evil and to guard them against error and sin, as well as a renunciation of false worship (if necessary), draw the attention of the catechumens to the real nature of Christian life, the struggle between flesh and spirit, the importance of self-denial, and the unending need for God's help.[40] After their election, the catechumens enter into a more intense period of purification and enlightenment. The scrutinies, prayers celebrated on several Sundays of Lent, "are meant to uncover, then heal all that is weak, defective, or sinful in the hearts of the elect; to bring out, then strengthen all that is upright, strong, and good . . . to deliver the elect from the power of sin and Satan, to protect them against temptation, and to give them strength in Christ, who is the way, the truth, and the life."[41] They are meant to "complete the conversion of the elect and deepen their resolve to hold fast to Christ and to carry out their decision to love God above all."[42] The catechumen is expected to repent of past sins and to abandon conduct or professions contrary to Christian faith and morals. In the early church, members of certain professions such as procurers, prostitutes, gladiators, charioteers, the makers of idols, actors, and soothsayers were excluded from Christian fellowship and participation in baptism.[43]

Finally, during the rite of baptism itself, the elect renounce sin, promise to reject the glamour of evil and to refuse to be mastered by sin, and reject Satan and all his works and empty promises in addition to professing faith in the Triune God. After baptism, the neophyte is clothed with a white baptismal garment signifying that he or she is a new creation and has been clothed in Christ.

Ethical instruction and exhortations are intrinsic to Christian initiation. The transition effected by the sacrament is described as rebirth and new creation, both indicating an altered state of existence. The mimetic reenactment of the death and resurrection of Christ in the immersion of the baptized literally puts to death the old man and raises up the new one. The

---

39. Christian Initiation of Adults, no. 42, in *The Rites of the Catholic Church*, vol. 1 (Collegeville, MN: Liturgical, 1990).

40. Ibid., no. 90.

41. Ibid., no. 141.

42. Ibid.

43. Everett, "Liturgy and Ethics: A Response to Saliers and Ramsey," 235.

first letter of Peter, traditionally viewed as a baptismal sermon, describes the new ethical life that is to accompany the new state of being:

> Like obedient children, do not be conformed to the desires that you formerly had in ignorance. Instead, as he who called you is holy, be holy yourselves in all your conduct; for it is written, "You shall be holy, for I am holy" . . . Now that you have purified your souls by your obedience to the truth so that you have genuine mutual love, love one another deeply from the heart. You have been born anew, not of perishable but of imperishable seed, through the living and enduring word of God . . . Rid yourselves, therefore, of all malice, and all guile, insincerity, envy, and all slander." (1 Pet 1:14–16, 22–23; 2:1)

In addition, a substantial portion of Colossians outlines the ethical requirements of the baptismal life (Col 2:12—3:17). The baptized are to put to death whatever is earthly: fornication, impurity, passion, evil desire, and greed, as well as anger, wrath, malice, slander, abusive language, and lies. These are to be replaced by compassion, kindness, humility, meekness, patience, and mutual forgiveness. The baptized are to clothe themselves in love and to let the peace of Christ rule in their hearts. They are to teach and admonish one another in all wisdom. Although baptism is much more than moral exhortation, it is at least that, an exhortation based on the new relationships with God and with one another forged in baptism.

Liturgy as ethical commitment effects a real change in an individual through the reception of baptism and Eucharist, a change that entails ethical actions in harmony with the new status of the person incorporated into Christ and his ecclesial body by way of these two sacraments. This ethical commitment is not extrinsic or forensic in the sense of an obligation undertaken in a juridical way, as when I commit myself to fulfill the terms of a contract. It is not just a decision to act in an ethical way, as when I commit myself to volunteer in a soup kitchen or to tithe. On the contrary, in this model, ethics follows being. Sacramental ontology creates a body, the ecclesial body of Christ. This body is conformed to Christ in the pattern of his death and resurrection, a conformity that entails an ethical obligation to ethical action according to that pattern. We discern that pattern within the ministerial life of Jesus.

Unity in Sacrament/Unity in Ethics

Having sketched out five models illustrating the relationship of ethics to liturgy, the remaining task is to examine how unity in sacrament relates to unity in ethics.

Liturgy as instrument of ethics creates an extrinsic relationship between liturgy and ethics. The liturgy is thematized to serve an ethical purpose, as in Masses for peace. The theme is arbitrary, often imposed on the liturgy from elsewhere, rather than being derived from the core of the rite itself. One ethical theme could easily be chosen over another. This is the weakest of all the relationships discussed here, because there is really no true or deep relationship between unity in one and unity in the other.

Liturgy as exemplar of ethics does not have a superimposed theme, as in the previous model, but it still features a somewhat extrinsic relationship between liturgy and ethics insofar as it offers something to be imitated. It is oriented to right action rather than the formation or ontology of the ethical subject. Such disunity between liturgy and ethical action simply means that the liturgy as exemplar has not been effective by being sufficiently convincing or has not been powerful enough to effect ethical change.

Liturgy as formative of moral character develops an intrinsic relationship between ethics and liturgy insofar as it is focused on the character of the ethical subject. Since moral character is formed by the liturgy, one presumes that only those who experience Christian liturgy are formed by it, hence the charge of communitarianism or sectarianism that that has been raised against this model.[44] While the liturgy in this instance can supply a specific Christian ethic, this ethic has no grounds for constituting in itself a universal ethic apart from the biblical narrative that informs it. Thus ethical actions within the liturgical community may differ from ethical actions outside this community. Serious ethical improprieties may sever an individual from the liturgical body, leading liturgically to literal excommunication, which removes the sinner from both the liturgical celebration and the ecclesial body. It is effectively liturgical shunning for the protection and purity of the liturgical community and the medicinal correction of the sinner. Outside the liturgical body and the biblical narrative that informs it, ethical pluralism remains a distinct possibility, and the liturgy has no way of informing this pluralism or critiquing it except to say that it is inconsistent with the values of a particular religious community.

44. Lisa Sowle Cahill, op. cit.

Liturgy as verification of ethics provides a religious motivation for an ethics that may be universal. In this model, it is not the specific moral action that is Christian; rather, a potentially universal moral ethic becomes a religious action insofar as it embodies the self-gift of an individual to God in response to God's initiative in first gifting himself in Jesus. In this model, sacrament is a passage whose modality is symbol in present time, and thus it is possible to celebrate in sacramental fullness an ethical life of agape that is perhaps only experienced sporadically and imperfectly in historical time. The agape of eucharistic communion, for instance, is sorely tested in the parking lot after the liturgy. Therefore, the liturgy may achieve an ideal that is only in the process of being realized in real historical time outside of the liturgy.

A morally divided body creates serious cognitive dissonance with the sacrament that represents the moral life in completion. The distance between sacramental fullness and experiential incompleteness shows the fullness that remains to be achieved. The sacrament serves as a critique of what is still lacking in the historical realization of ethical values, although ethical disunity does not necessarily break the unity of the sacramental body. Rather, the failure within ethical living finds no verification in the liturgy and therefore is identified as an inauthentic way of life.

In the *liturgy as commitment* model, ethical failure violates baptismal promises and the unity of the body constituted eucharistically. Serious ethical misconduct potentially fractures the unity of the body on account of the intrinsic bond between the unity of the body constituted sacramentally and ethical action that conforms to the body. If function follows form, and action follows identity, then deviant activity must flow from a different identity than that constituted sacramentally.

The same question must be asked in the context of sacramental ontology as with character ethics: is this a communitarian ethic with its consequent danger of sectarianism? Does this ethic possess any potential of relating to a universal ethic? The answer to this lies not in ethics, but in ecclesiology, and whether that ecclesiology is exclusivist or inclusivist in admitting relationships of perfect and imperfect communion with other Christians and, potentially, with non-Christians. Here it is not only a question of synthesizing the two theological disciplines of liturgy and ethics, but also of soteriology and anthropology, and how the unity of the ecclesial body is related to the unity of the whole human race. The question becomes no longer the relationship between ethics and liturgy or even between

ethics and the unity of the church, but between ethics and the authentically human, and how the authentically human is related to the ecclesial
community.

6

Grace and the Good Life: Why the God of the Gospel Cares How We Live

David Yeago

WE ARE GATHERED HERE to consider theologically the church-dividing potential of conflicts over moral teaching. The conference announcement asserts: "We have little sense of just when and how ethical disputes rightly impact communion within and among the churches." I take this to mean two things, perhaps: that we do not have much conceptual clarity about the relationship of moral teaching and church unity, but also, more immediately, that we are perplexed about how to proceed amidst the "ethical disputes" of which the statement speaks, that we do not see clearly the path of faithfulness.

My goal in this paper is primarily to address the first concern, to increase our clarity of vision about what is at stake in moral dispute among Christians. Indeed, I want to make only one very narrow point, though I shall sketch out a rather wide theological trajectory in making it. I want to address, from a somewhat different angle, a matter mentioned by Professor Jenson in his keynote lecture: the claim that Christians have a unity "in Christ" or "in the gospel" that is somehow impervious even to very substantial disagreement about moral questions. I'm speaking here not of the deep ontological unity founded by baptism, but about the concord in faith and teaching that is necessary for church-fellowship. Amidst the ethical turmoil of the denominations, voices are continually heard insisting that if we agree about Christ, other disagreements are not decisive. Agreement about Christ may in some quarters be described in terms of Nicene Orthodoxy; among Lutherans, one is likely to hear that if we agree about the gospel, we need not agree about the law.

The thesis I want to argue is that we *cannot* agree about Christ if we disagree about substantial matters of moral teaching. To suppose that we can implies serious misconceptions of Christ. I am not arguing, in Professor Jenson's terms, that every ethical dispute is simultaneously doctrinal. Rather I am arguing that agreement about Christ cannot be only doctrinal. In more traditional theological terms, the proposition is that the relationship between Jesus Christ and the law of God is such that we cannot agree in teaching about Christ if we disagree substantially about the law.

To be sure, the phrase "disagree substantially" papers over a large question: How do we know which moral disagreements are substantial? Treasure what Professor Jenson said in answer to that question on Monday night, for I am going to give you no help whatsoever in answering it. The bet I'm making is that by the end of the lecture you will find that it was worthwhile to concentrate as narrowly on this one point as I am going to do.

In his late work, *On the Councils and the Church*, Martin Luther argued that the so-called antinomians of his day, who taught that the law of God had no place in the church's teaching, were making what was at bottom a *christological* mistake.

> For there is no such Christ that died for sinners who do not, after the forgiveness of sins, desist from sins and lead a new life . . . [The Antinomians] may be fine Easter preachers, but they are very poor Pentecost preachers, for they do not preach *de sanctificatione et vivificatione Spiritus Sancti*, "about sanctification by the Holy Spirit," but only about redemption by Jesus Christ, although Christ (whom they extol so highly, and rightly so) is *Christ*, that is, he has purchased redemption from sin and death so that the Holy Spirit might transform us out of the old Adam into new people . . . Now whoever does not abstain from sin, but persists in an evil life, must have a different Christ, that of the Antinomians; the *real* Christ is not there, even if all the angels should cry, "Christ! Christ!"[1]

---

1. Luther, *On the Councils*, LW 41:114. Translation altered and emphasis added.

I am not concerned today with whether or not Luther was being quite fair to his old student-turned-adversary Johannes Agricola in these words, nor do I claim that our contemporary moral disputes are simple replays of the antinomian controversy. Though there certainly seems to be a good bit of antinomianism out there, I don't charge the people who disagree with me in our present debates (or, for that matter, Agricola) with teaching "that we should not abstain from sin but may persist in an evil life."

I am concerned rather with a wider implication of what Luther says here: that *disputes about divine law involve, in the end, disputes about Jesus Christ, and therefore disputes about the gospel.* I want to explore briefly with you what understanding of divine law and what understanding of Jesus Christ as Savior might underlie such a conviction, not as an exercise in Luther interpretation, but in what might be called a dogmatic inquiry, a consideration of the truth of things in the light of Holy Scripture.

Divine Law in the Context of Creation

Let me start out, however, with a formulation from the Reformation era. According to the Lutheran *Formula of Concord*, the law of God is "properly a divine teaching in which the righteous, unchanging will of God has revealed how human beings are to be disposed in their nature, thoughts, words, and deeds so that they may be pleasing and acceptable to God."[2] This definition, which isn't peculiarly Lutheran in any distinctive way, places the law of God within the widest possible horizon, because it relates the law of God to the righteous, unchanging will of God.

This kind of talk has a scriptural background; it refers to the will of the Father that our Lord taught us to pray may be done on earth as it is in heaven, that will to which our Lord dedicated himself in the Garden of Gethsemane in the face of death and his own natural human shrinking from death. It does not refer to a mere discrete sum of divine appointments but to a coherent purpose that embraces the whole creation. Thus, the Letter to the Ephesians speaks of the "mystery of God's will" which embraces all things in heaven and on earth, and works itself out in an *oikonomia*, a plan that moves all things towards a final reconfiguration and unification in Christ (Eph 1:9–10).

---

2. *FC*, Solid Declaration 5/17. My translation from BSELK; Kolb-Wengert mistranslates here.

The law of God is a teaching from God in which this righteous unchanging will of God makes itself known *in a certain respect*, with regard to "how human beings are to be disposed in their nature, thoughts, words, and deeds so that they may be pleasing and acceptable to God."[3] What is at stake here is clearly more than a sum of rules for behavior, a list of dos and don'ts. God's law bears not only on our actions, not only on our thoughts and words, but even on our *nature*. It calls for a certain way of *being*, a disposition of the self at its deepest roots. God wants us to *exist* in this way; otherwise, His purpose is not fulfilled in us and God is not satisfied with us.

Divine law thus understood cries out for explication in terms of the doctrine of creation. The God of whom the Bible speaks is not connected to the world by any bond of necessity. He relates to the world in utter freedom, in the freedom that He *is* in his eternal fullness as Father, Son, and Holy Spirit. The freedom that the Triune God *is*, is the freedom of love; it is freedom always eternally realized as love, and love utterly free to be only and always itself. There is thus nothing needy in God's love, and nothing arbitrary in His freedom.[4]

Creation springs from the mystery of this utterly free love. God does not need to create, nor does He gain from creating. From sheer existence on, creation is pure gravy for the creature, pure inexplicable benefit. Why is there anything other than God, why not just Father, Son, and Holy Spirit existing in an eternal, living, and boundless plenitude of life? Certainly giving being to others is a thoroughly *appropriate* thing for a God who is love to do, but there seems to be no sufficient *motivation* for him to do it rather than not do it.[5] I can't improve on Margaret Anscombe's formulation: we can only say that God must have created the world "out of sheer exuberance."[6]

---

3. The law is therefore not the revelation of the *whole* of the divine will; the heart of the mystery, which has to do with Christ, remains concealed until the Holy Spirit makes it known by the apostolic preaching of the gospel. Cf. Rom 16:25–27; 1 Cor 2:6–13; Eph 3:12; Col 1:24—2:3.

4. The terms of this account of God's freedom and love are borrowed from Karl Barth, *Church Dogmatics* 2/1.

5. Cf. Michael Liccione, "Mystery and Explanation," *Thomist* 59 (1995) 223–45, for a good account of the distinction between the intelligible and fitting *reason* for God's creating and the unfathomable mystery of his *motive* for actually doing it. The point turns on the recognition that there are many things that an agent might have a good reason to do, things that would be *appropriate* to do, which are nevertheless not done because the agent lacks sufficient *motivation* to do them rather than not do them.

6. Cited by Liccione in ibid., 245.

Nevertheless, creation glorifies God, even though it does not add to Him. Indeed, it glorifies Him precisely *because* it does not benefit Him. This is why we can say that creating is an appropriate thing for God to do, even if we can never understand why He actually went and did it. A God who gained for Himself by creating would not be the free and majestic God proclaimed by Holy Scripture. That God creates as sheer gift and benefit to the creature is precisely what glorifies God as utterly free and infinitely living love. This is in a way a founding insight of Christian theology; it is captured in the famous statement of St. Irenaeus that "the glory of God is a living human being"[7]—that is, a human creature living and flourishing, fully enjoying the goodness that the living God has exuberantly extended to creatures.

I belabor this point because it is critically important for the understanding of divine law. There is a deplorable tendency, sometimes ascribed to the church and sometimes, unfortunately, found in churches, to suppose that God gives law to human creatures chiefly in order to show them who's in charge. It's as though the *content* of the commandments was less important than the *sheer fact of the imposed constraint* that presses human beings to acknowledge their inferior status before God. This constraint then easily comes to be perceived as oppressive and inherently degrading, something from which we need to be delivered, whether by therapy or atheism or antinomian religion. But this can't be what God's law is all about; a god who had anything to *prove* to human beings could only be one of the tin pot gods of the heathen, not the Lord God of the Bible.

It is of course important, to say the least, that we recognize that *God is God and we are not.* But it is not important because God needs our acknowledgment. It's important for us, because not glorifying God as God, in St. Paul's terms, makes us fools.[8] It delivers us to a self-inflicted blindness in which we stumble about and eventually come to grief on rocks of reality that we, individually and collectively, refuse to see. In short, it produces something like human history and human life as we know them, or as the diagnostic tools given us in Holy Scripture enable us to see them.

Pope John Paul II summed up with beautiful precision the true meaning of the law as the word of our Creator: "God, who alone is good, knows perfectly what is good for man, and by virtue of his very love proposes

7. Irenaeus, *Against Heresies* IV, 20.

8. Cf. Rom 1:19–23.

this good to man in the commandments"[9] Human creatures, along with the angels, occupy a distinctive place in God's purpose as Creator: as I learned from Robert Jenson long ago, God, in summoning the world into existence, not only speaks *about* these creatures; He speaks *to* them. He has chosen and designed them to be partners with him in a communion of life and love. In keeping with this purpose, God not only has a good thing in mind for human creatures, He *proposes* this good to them, and calls them to embrace their good in their own created freedom. We are indeed called to acknowledge God as God by His commandments, but concretely that means acknowledging His wisdom and goodness, trusting that God does indeed know what is good for us so that by walking in His ways we will walk in blessing.

The Socratic question about the good life, the happy or blessed life, is thus by no means simply alien to the Bible. The Bible is not a book about duty (as modernist Protestantism sometimes supposed) for which a question about happiness would be a self-indulgent impertinence. The ancient Greek question about the good life was in any case never a question about happiness in the sense of subjective good feelings. It was the question of what kind of life is good for beings of a certain kind, the kind of beings we simply are and did not choose to be.[10] The medical analogy is both traditional and illuminating. Easy carbs and lots of sugar may make me feel good—for a while. But they are not good for me, and constant indulgence in them will harm me. This is so whether I like it or not; I have a certain kind of body that works in a particular way, and this fact is prior and impervious to my wishing and craving.

The ancient question about the good life transfers these terms to our existence as *persons* capable of reflection and choice. I cannot decide what is good for me as a person anymore than I can simply decree that donuts and pie will make my body healthy. We may feel good when we do evil, but evildoing rots the soul as surely as sugar causes tooth decay. That's why the good life is at the same time the *reasonable* life, the kind of life that makes sense for human beings.

At least at certain levels of tradition, but not simply under some sort of late and malign Hellenistic influence, the Old Testament quite

---

9. Pope John Paul II, *Veritatis Splendor* §35.

10. On the idea of the good life in ancient Greek ethics, especially Aristotle, cf. Henry Veatch, *Rational Man: A Modern Interpretation of Aristotelian Ethics* (Indianapolis: Liberty Fund, 2003; orig. ed. 1962).

self-consciously presents the Torah as the answer to the question about the good life. Thus in the first Psalm: "Blessed/happy is the person who walks not in the counsel of the wicked, nor stands in the way of sinners, nor sits in the seat of scoffers; but his delight is in the law of the LORD, and on his law he meditates day and night" (Ps 1:1–2 RSV).

The Old Testament is likewise quite clear that this blessed life is the only *reasonable* life. Law and wisdom, practical know-how, are closely linked; if the word of the Lord made the heavens and the earth, it only makes sense that those who are out of joint with His word are out of joint with reality.[11] For the law is precisely the word of our Creator proposing to us what is good for us.

Whatever else needs to be said about the tortured history of humankind with God's law, this fundamental point should never be obscured: the law is, as St. Paul acknowledges, holy, just, and good (Rom 7:12). In itself it is a beneficent word, a word ordered *eis zoēn* (Rom 7:9) to life, to that "living" of the human creature that glorifies God. If what is ordered to life has become death to me, the problem is in *me*; I need to be delivered from the sin that dwells in me and takes the commandment as the occasion to bring about my death (cf. Rom 7:11). Whatever it means to be "free from the law," therefore, it cannot mean freedom from the unchanging righteous will of my Creator; that would mean freedom from my good, freedom from *life*. There is a name for that kind of freedom in the Christian vocabulary: it's called Hell.

The Law of God and the *Imago Dei*

Now we come to a significant moment in our reflections, a hinge on which much turns. If God's law proposes to human beings the good for which God created them, then the divine law necessarily has an inner, material connection to the *image and likeness* of God, in or according to which God fashioned the human creature, according to Genesis 1:26–27.[12] In its immediate context, this notion seems to be related to the authority God gives

11. Notice how the cosmic Wisdom-poem in Proverbs 8:22–31 leads directly to the exhortation in 8:32: "And now, my children, listen to me: happy are those who keep my ways" (RSV alt).

12. By an "inner, material" connection, I mean that the two notions are not necessarily connected in the ways that strictly historical-critical inquiry can describe, as though the one notion grew out of or influenced the other; I mean that they are connected by virtue of their *content*.

to the human creature over the rest of creation; bearing God's image, made in His likeness, the human creature is to rule over the other creatures as God's viceroy and partner. "In the image of God" is therefore also descriptive of the good purpose for which God made humankind, and thus has an inherent connection with the law of God.

Genesis 1 does not tell us much about the content of the divine image, but the idea is taken up and developed elsewhere in Holy Scripture. In order to avoid certain old controversies about the *imago Dei*, let me say that it certainly involves the distinctive being of human creatures as persons, impelled by what we are to seek the truth and desire the good. But the idea is not complete without reference to the "true holiness and righteousness" that, according to Ephesians (4:23–24), characterize the human being who is created *kata theon*, "in accord with God." Conversely, that the will of God expressed in commandments intends that we be conformed to God's own holiness and goodness is also recognized in Scripture. "Say to all the congregation of the people of Israel, You shall be holy; for I the LORD your God am holy" (Lev 19:2 RSV; cf. also 20:7). Likewise Jesus, commanding love of enemies, refers to God's goodness even to the evil and the unjust, and concludes: "Be perfect, therefore, as your heavenly Father is perfect" (Matt 5:48 NRSV)—that is, be complete and full in your love, as your Father is full and complete in love.

But idea of the *imago Dei* is also developed *christologically* in the New Testament. In 2 Corinthians, St. Paul writes that believers see in a certain way[13] the glory of the Lord and are being transformed into the image of what they see (2 Cor 3:18). Later, he identifies the image of God with Christ himself, whose glorious gospel brings light (cf. 4:4); it is God who says, "Let the light shine in the darkness" when the gospel is preached, so that we see "the light of the knowledge of the glory of God" precisely in the face of Jesus Christ (4:6). In Romans, God's purpose with those who are called by the gospel is that they be "conformed to the image of His Son, so that He might be the first-born of many brothers and sisters" (Rom 8:28–29).

In the theological tradition, moreover, the characterization of Christ as God's image has been closely tied to the Johannine identification of Christ as the Word of God who was with God and was God, already at creation (John 1:1–3). The association is not haphazard but arises from the Johannine account itself. When this Word becomes flesh and dwells among us, we behold glory in him (v. 14), the Father's glory in the Son; he is, so to

---

13. This "in a certain way" covers over the formidable exegetical difficulty of 2 Corinthians 3:7–17; the point made here is, I think, capable of standing on its own.

speak, the exegesis to us of the invisible Father (v. 18). He himself declares to his disciples: "Whoever has seen me, has seen the Father" (John 14:9). The material convergence of the Johannine Word with the Pauline Image is unmistakable.

Reflecting on these interchanges within the canon, the seventeenth-century Lutheran theologian Johann Gerhard sketched out the connections between law, image of God, and Christ in terms that I shall save myself trouble and borrow, since they seem to me simply right.[14] According to Gerhard:

> From eternity, God the Father has begotten the Son, in whom his image shines out fully and perfectly . . . Even though he has eternally begotten this image, his Son, yet on account of his overflowing goodness he willed that another image exist, in this case not substantial but accidental;[15] therefore he created the human being (as well as the angels) "according to his image and likeness" (Genesis 1:27), which, according to the Apostle, is to be defined by true righteousness and holiness (Ephesians 4:24). On account of the image of God shining out in them, human beings were conformed to their Creator. (106)

For Gerhard, the *law* is a "mirror of divine righteousness, holiness, and perfection," a kind of counterpart and reflection of the *imago Dei* in human beings. Because human beings are to affirm this image in freedom, God *describes* it to them. God sets before the human creature "another image of his righteousness and holiness in the law itself, for what God wills that we be in the law, free from every stain of sin and gleaming with the true light of righteousness and holiness, is what he himself is, though in a manner far more perfect, or rather utterly singular" (106).

In light of the fall of humankind into sin, the relationship of the created image of God and its description in the law to the eternal Image, the Son, becomes critically important. Again Gerhard: "Since on the basis of

---

14. Gerhard, *Loci Theologici*, ed. Eduard Preuss (Berlin: Schlawitz, 1865), vol. 3, *Locus XII de Lege Dei* §206. All citations from Gerhard are from this section; page citations to the Preuss edition will be given in parentheses in the text.

I should mention that nothing in what Gerhard says here seem to me to be peculiarly or divisively Lutheran; it is certainly grounded in Patristic insights about the *imago Dei.*

15. The *imago Dei* in the human creature is accidental in the sense that human beings can lose it without ceasing to be human. Reformation theologians relate the *imago* primarily to "true righteousness and holiness" and therefore speak of it as "lost" at the fall, without denying that the created human presuppositions for righteousness and holiness continue to be present in fallen human beings.

the law [fallen] human beings were not able to climb up to the restoration of the image of God in themselves by their own powers, therefore God sent his Son into the world. Since he is the substantial image of God the Father by reason of the divine nature, he was able to set forth the image of God in the flesh he assumed in an utterly perfect way, and to restore that image in us through faith and the Spirit of new life" (106–7).

For this reason, Gerhard says, "the holy life of Christ is the most perfect rule of piety and all the virtues, for whatever the law prescribes outwardly shone forth in the heart of Christ; all his actions and all his words corresponded with complete exactness to the norm of divine law" (107). Thus Christ and the law are in a certain way unified in terms of the image of God: the law describes the holiness and righteousness of which the essential divine Word and Image is the archetype, the holiness and righteousness concretely realized for our redemption in a human way in the person of the Word and Image incarnate, Jesus Christ.

The Pauline Critique of the Law

This may seem a strangely cozy account of Christ and the law, especially coming from one Lutheran by way of another. What about the Apostle Paul and his apparent polarization of law and grace, law and Christ? As many of you know, this whole issue has been a matter of hot contention in New Testament studies for several decades; I first encountered the controversy in seminary when I was assigned to write a paper on Sanders' *Paul and Palestinian Judaism* in the early 1980s. Since then, of the writing of book reports on Sanders there has been no end.[16] The so-called New Perspective has contested not only a narrowly "Lutheran" reading of Paul, as the rhetoric suggests, but the whole Western tradition of theological Pauline interpretation going back to Augustine. The New Perspective has at times seemed to command the field, though counterattacks have not ceased and seem at present to be growing in frequency and intensity.

16. E. P. Sanders, *Paul and Palestinian Judaism: A Comparison of Patterns of Religion* (Philadelphia: Fortress, 1977). For an accessible presentation of one influential New Perspective reading of Paul, see N. T. Wright, *Paul in Fresh Perspective* (Minneapolis: Fortress, 2009). For a balanced overview and critique of the New Perspective, cf. Stephen Westerholm, *Perspectives New and Old on Paul: The "Lutheran" Paul and His Critics* (Grand Rapids: Eerdmans, 2003). I have found particularly insightful the second thoughts of a New Perspective pioneer, Francis Watson, in *Paul and the Hermeneutics of Faith* (Edinburgh: T. & T. Clark, 2004).

You will be glad to know that I realize that I cannot go into those debates here. Let me simply propose a very brief three-point summary of what I believe broadly to be the case.

First, it is clearly right (as the New Perspective has emphasized) that the immediate practical occasion of Paul's engagement of this issue is the Gentile mission and the admission of Gentiles into the people of God of the Last Days.

Second, looking at the matter in this apocalyptic horizon, Paul takes the *theological* question at stake to be: What is the way to eschatological life, to deliverance from wrath in the final judgment? Thus, in Paul's framing of the question, he has already taken it beyond the original occasion. Paul argues that however true in principle it may be, according to Leviticus, that the person who keeps God's statutes and ordinances will "live" by them (Lev 18:5, LXX), in concrete actuality, given the grip of evil desire on the human heart, the *last* word must be that of Habakkuk 2:4b: "The one who is righteous *by faith* shall live."[17] Life—eschatological life, deliverance on the Last Day—is found only by adhering to Christ, being joined to him in such a way that he lives in us (Gal 2:20), and dying and rising with him (Rom 6:1–11)—all of which is contained in Paul's understanding of the phrase "by faith."

Third and finally, I would argue that the Augustinian tradition is right to discern that Paul has so dealt with *his* question as to exclude by rather direct implication *any* account of the way to eschatological life that does not direct our trust and hope exclusively to God's grace and mercy in Jesus Christ.[18]

What one cannot find in St. Paul is any suggestion that grace and the gospel stand over against the law as the *abrogation* of God's will that we be

17. On the exegetical and theological issues behind this summary, cf. Watson, *Paul and the Hermeneutics of Faith*, 33–77.

18. Cf. the consensus on this point in the Lutheran-Roman Catholic *Joint Declaration on the Doctrine of Justification*: "We also share the conviction that the message of justification directs us in a special way towards the heart of the New Testament witness to God's saving action in Christ: it tells us that as sinners our new life is solely due to the forgiving and renewing mercy that God imparts as a gift and we receive in faith, and never can merit in any way" (par. 17). The phrase "message of justification" refers specifically in context to the (mostly Pauline) *New Testament* teaching on justification; the statement in effect articulates a shared Augustinian perception of the theological and pastoral significance of Paul's discourse of justification and righteousness.

truly righteous and holy. On the contrary, he argues that it is only through grace and the gospel that God *achieves* this purpose.

Consider the movement from Romans 5 to Romans 6. Paul has been magnifying the grace of God, which takes human wrong only as the occasion further to display his goodness: "Where sin increased, grace abounded all the more, so that, as sin reigned in death, grace also might reign through righteousness to eternal life through Jesus Christ our Lord" (Rom 5:21 RSV).

Paul supposes that someone might respond to this exultation with a stupid question: "Shall we just keep on sinning, then, and give grace even more opportunity to abound?" (cf. 6:1). His response, in essence, is that the questioner is forgetting that "grace" is not an abstract attitude of acceptance or a merely formal pardon. Grace has a face and a name: Jesus Christ. To be grasped by this grace is to die with Christ so that we might live a new kind of life in him (cf. 6:3-4). To reckon with this grace is to reckon ourselves dead to sin and alive to God through Jesus Christ (6:11).

Thus the apostle's exposition of God's grace moves seamlessly from the language of dying and rising with Christ (6:2-11) to the language of lordship and service (6:12-23)—and notice what he says: "For sin will not master you, for you are not under law but under grace" (Rom 6:14, my translation). It is *because* Christians are not under the law but under grace that sin cannot master them. This statement only makes sense in light of what precedes it; "under grace" means for Paul "united with the Messiah in his dying and rising."

The point is clarified further at the beginning of Romans 8. Summing up the analysis in chapter 7, Paul says that the problem with the law is that it is "weak"—it cannot accomplish God's purpose; it cannot give the life to which it is nonetheless ordered.[19] It has been weakened, in fact, by "the flesh," that is, by *us*, by our debility as sinners (cf. 8:3). The law is subverted by sin, which has filled us with all kinds of wrong desire (cf. 7:8-12). We need deliverance, not from the burden of God's demands, but from the inward corruption that renders God's commandments burdensome. "Who will rescue me from the body of this death?" (7:24)—that is, at least in large part, who will rescue me from myself?[20]

19. This may seem surprising; we are perhaps more likely to think that the problem with the law is that it comes on too strong and overburdens us. But the apostle sees it otherwise. The very fact that the law, faced with our sin, can only accuse and condemn is the mark of its weakness; for it is not God's purpose to accuse and condemn.

20. I would not dismiss the possibility, given the full reach of Paul's understanding of the body, that "the body of this death" might also involve our bodily entanglement in

God has rescued us, Paul replies, by sending his Son in the likeness of sinful flesh (8:3). In doing so, he has accomplished what the law could not accomplish: the fulfillment *in us* of what the law righteously demands (8:4). Paul goes on to speak of this in an intricate tangle of language in which the gift of the Holy Spirit is correlated with belonging to Christ and Christ's presence "in" the believer (cf. 8:9–11), so that the flesh may be overcome.

These are deep waters, but for our purposes one point is crucial. By sending His Son, God *achieves* His purpose for creation and for human creatures. The grace of God in Jesus Christ means that sin will not master us; through this grace God has brought about the fulfillment of the law *within* us. To paraphrase John Paul II, "God, who alone is good, knows perfectly what is good for human creatures, and by virtue of his very love *bestows* this good on humankind in Jesus Christ."[21] What the law proposes, therefore, the gospel bestows; the law tells us about life, while the gospel, because it sets forth Christ, actually puts the bread of life on the table.

Agreement in Christ and Moral Disputes

We can see now, I believe, that substantial agreement about Christ *must* involve substantial agreement about the law. Christ is in person the *lex impleta*, the fulfilled law, for us and on our behalf, so that in Christ righteousness is not bypassed but realized, becomes actual and available for us. *He could not be our Savior otherwise*, for the righteousness demanded by the law is our only possible well-being. Our unity in Christ is therefore in its substance unity in righteousness, unity in the eschatological fulfillment of the law. Therefore, we cannot say who Christ is and how he is "for us" if we cannot say what righteousness is. The knowledge of Jesus Christ is therefore not only what we might call doctrinal knowledge, but is inherently also

---

distorted patterns of corporate life in this present age; but in Romans 7, he seems to focus on the wrong desire within the person.

21. Let me be clear that this variation is not intended as a Protestant *riposte* to the Pope's original formulation. I take it as a claim with which he would have been in agreement. Cf. the profound statement in *Redemptor Hominis*, par. 9: "The redemption of the world—this tremendous mystery of love in which creation is renewed—is, at its deepest root, the fullness of righteousness in a human Heart—the Heart of the First-born Son—in order that it may become righteousness in the hearts of many human beings, predestined from eternity in the First-born Son to be children of God and called to grace, called to love." Translation altered; the official translation renders *iustitia* as "justice" rather than "righteousness," which I regard as misleading.

knowledge of a *way* that Christians are summoned and privileged to walk, recognition of the good kind of life that we receive from Jesus Christ.[22]

If this is the case, then it should come as no surprise that morally divided Christians turn out to be unable to engage together in basic practices of the church's life mission. In the Evangelical Lutheran Church in America, we have declared that we have no common teaching about homosexuality. We are now beginning to realize that as a result, we can no longer catechize together, because we cannot teach the Ten Commandments together. Even on this seemingly small point, difficulties abound. Can congregations that have taught their children the *Catechism* together continue to do so? We now have to say: "Maybe, maybe not." Will the denomination be able to produce instructional materials that all congregations can use in good conscience? The probable answer is no.

The question about catechesis was one of the very first questions that I heard from ELCA pastors in the immediate aftermath of the ELCA Assembly last year. This surprised me at first, but I soon realized that it expressed a sound pastoral instinct. After all, in the Lutheran tradition, core catechesis has never been only instruction in the doctrine of justification by faith, or even in the content of the Apostles' Creed. Justification is not even mentioned in the *Small Catechism*, and the exposition of the creed is framed by instruction in the Ten Commandments and the Lord's Prayer and followed by expositions of the sacraments. In its full form, the *Catechism* also contains scriptural guidance for various stations in life, as well as forms for morning and evening prayer, prayer at mealtime, and liturgies for baptism

---

22. Having written the foregoing, it occurs to me that what I have set forth is a kind of shorthand version of a less easily summarized claim: that the Christ who saves us is *the Christ attested in Holy Scripture*. Knowing the real Christ (in Luther's terms) involves a close engagement with the manifold witness to Jesus Christ in the New Testament, but likewise a reading of the testimony to Jesus in light of the Old Testament (which the New Testament already demands), without which we cannot know what the term "Christ"(Messiah) *means*. The foundational church dogma, arrived at in conflict with the Gnostics and Marcion, that the God who sent Jesus the Savior is the same God who created the material world and gave the law to Moses, was simultaneously and inseparably a claim about God, a claim about how Christ may be known, and instruction in reading the Scriptures. The kind of dogmatic exposition I have given here will remain formalistic and inert if it does not point us to the long, never-in-this-life-concluded journey of detailed engagement with the Scriptures to find Jesus Christ. If the preached word and the sacraments are the sacramental means of Christ's availability to us, one might say that the Scriptures are the sacrament of his *identity*, his particularity. Cf. on this J. Todd Billings, *The Word of God for the People of God: An Entryway to the Theological Interpretation of Scripture* (Grand Rapids: Eerdmans, 2010).

and the blessing of marriage.[23] The *Small Catechism* is thus inescapably an introduction to a distinctive way of life[24] under the redeeming lordship of Jesus Christ, confessed at its theological center, the exposition of the Second Article of the Creed.[25]

By inflicting severe damage on our capacity to guide catechumens into this way of life together, the 2009 ELCA Assembly actions have impaired the communion of ELCA congregations with one another. It is worth remembering Michael Root's diagnostic question to determine whether two or more groups of churches have the agreement necessary for ecclesial communion: "Can they perform together regularly and in a comprehensive range of situations the activities either considers essential to the identity of the church as church without violating either's understanding of the identity of the church?"[26] Christians divided by substantial moral disagreement will *always* find that the answer to this question is no, just as we in the ELCA woke up one August morning to discover that we must now answer, "No."

The reason for this is essentially christological, as I have tried to suggest. Moral disagreement does not impair church fellowship because God

23. For these additional elements, cf. *The Book of Concord: The Confessions of the Evangelical Lutheran Church*, ed. Robert Kolb and Timothy J. Wengert (Minneapolis: Fortress, 2000) 363–73.

24. Luther himself clearly understood the *Catechism* in this way: "Although no one can or should force another person to believe, nevertheless one should insist upon and hold the masses to this: that they know what is right and wrong among those among whom they wish to reside, eat, and earn a living. For example, if people want to live in a particular city, they ought to know and abide by the laws of the city whose protection they enjoy, no matter whether they believe or are at heart scoundrels and villains." Martin Luther, preface to the *Small Catechism*, in Kolb and Wengert, eds., *The Book of Concord*, 349.

25. "I believe that Jesus Christ, true God, begotten of the Father in eternity, and also a true human being, born of the Virgin Mary, is my Lord. He has redeemed me, a lost and condemned human being. He has purchased and freed me from all sins, from death, and from the power of the devil, not with gold or silver but with his holy, precious blood and with his innocent suffering and death. He has done all this in order that I may belong to him, live under him in his kingdom, and serve him in eternal righteousness, innocence, and blessedness, just as he is risen from the dead and lives and rules eternally." Kolb and Wengert, eds., *The Book of Concord*, 355. This concentrated summary of the knowledge of Christ is itself a model in its recognition that knowing Christ involves knowing what it means to "live under him and his kingdom, and serve him."

26. Michael Root, "Identity and Difference: The Ecumenical Problem," in *Theology and Dialogue: Essays in Conversation with George Lindbeck*, ed. Bruce Marshall (Notre Dame: Notre Dame University Press, 1990) 165–90; here 181.

remains angrily demanding despite the gospel, or because someone is putting the law in place of the gospel; it happens because the gospel itself is the good news that in Jesus Christ, God has achieved His purpose in creating the world, His intention to bless us and do us good. "I have come that they might have life, and have it abundantly," says our Lord (John 10:10). And *life* is just what the law of God describes.

7

Learning How to Be Morally Divided: *Evangelicals and Catholics Together* in the Morally Divided Body

James J. Buckley

How does the group "Evangelicals and Catholics Together" (ECT) help us address the theme, "The Morally Divided Body: Ethical Disagreement and the Disunity of the Church" set for this conference of the Center for Catholic and Evangelical Theology (CCET)? I will begin by proposing a way Catholics and Evangelicals need to learn to be morally divided and have ethical disagreements in a culture that pressures us to choose between what have (or has) traditionally been called "faith and morals."[1] Then, given this context, I will describe the origins of ECT, how I got involved, and what I see at stake in the contributions of "Evangelicals and Catholics Together." Specifically, does ECT help or hinder us in the effort to learn how to be

1. I will not pursue the history of this distinction—not only of "faith" from "morals" but even more importantly "faith and morals" from . . . what? The distinction has functioned in several different ways—an exegetical distinction among verses or parts of the Bible, between parts of Paul's letters, between sections within standard Greek and Latin manuals of doctrine, and then between two *branches of* theology—eventually separated into two *kinds of* theology by (according to Jaroslav Pelikan) Georg Calixtus in the seventeenth century. Jaroslav Pelikan, *The Emergence of the Catholic Tradition (100–600)* (Chicago: University of Chicago Press, 1971) 2–3. I use "ethical" and "moral" synonymously, but see note 51 below.

morally divided, or keep or make "faith and morals" whole? Finally, I will make three recommendations about how ECT could continue to address our theme in the future.

The advantage of this strategy of setting a context for ECT before interpreting it is that this context locates ECT outside itself, putting ECT in conversation with other Evangelical and Catholic projects. The disadvantage is that I will not offer anything close to a comprehensive description or evaluation of ECT. I hope the advantages outweigh the disadvantages.

Is There a Christian Morality?

Consider two problems with our moral divisions and ethical disagreements that at least some ordinary Christians face. On the one hand, to quote John Paul II, "an opinion is frequently heard which questions the intrinsic and unbreakable bond between faith and morality, as if membership in the Church and her internal unity were to be decided on the basis of faith as such [*fidei tantum*], while in the sphere of morality a pluralism of opinions and of kinds of behavior could be tolerated, these being left to the judgment of the individual subjective conscience or to the diversity of social and cultural contexts."[2] I will call this position "moral (or ethical) pluralism" or, polemically, "relativism." Our moral divisions and ethical disagreements would be, on this view, something quite separate from faith. Faith might be the anchor in the midst of such moral pluralism. But morality is a separate sphere from faith, a sphere of subjective conscience, or diverse cultural contexts.

On a second hand, on hearing of moral divisions and ethical disagreements, other plain persons may well think that we know very well what it means to be "moral" or "ethical," including how to be morally divided and disagree ethically. One form of this "moral (or ethical) foundationalism" or, polemically, "moralism" that is particularly important for North Americans is what Robert Bellah over forty years ago called "civil religion in America." Bellah argued that "there actually exists alongside of and rather clearly differentiated from the churches an elaborate and well-institutionalized civil religion in America."[3] He did not mean civil religion "as a form of national

2. John Paul II, *The Splendor of Truth*, #4 (similarly at #88ff.); Latin and English and other languages available at vatican.va (quoted here by paragraph number). The official English translation (which I revise above) at vatican.va of "fides tantum" is "faith alone."

3. Robert N. Bellah, "Civil Religion in America," *Dædalus* 96 (1967) 1–21 (here p. 1).

self-worship but as the subordination of the nation to ethical principles that transcend it in terms of which it should be judged."[4] On this view "moral division" and "ethical disagreement" are divisions over ethical principles that we use to judge ourselves or our nation—or, as things go global, the world. Here, instead of faith providing the anchor or refuge against a pluralism of subjects or cultures, morality provides a firm foundation for faith—or, if not for faith, at least for religious freedom. Bellah's claim has spawned an unfinished conversation among historians and political scientists as well as philosophers and theologians, and I only wish to raise up a small slice of this ongoing debate. I am thinking of the brand of American civil religion exemplified in those who might bemoan the impracticality of the many Catholic-Evangelical agreements reached thus far on any number of topics. They may be delighted to hear that Catholics and Evangelicals are finally getting down to business by facing up to our moral divisions and ethical disagreements—just as moral pluralists may worry that we are interfering with their morality or ethics.

You can perhaps sense here something of a piece of a culture war between (to continue engaging in some name-calling) moral relativists and moralists. On both views, the ancient distinction between "faith and morals" becomes a divide, with "faith" providing the foundation for (or alternative to) "morals" or "morals" providing the foundation for (or alternative to) "faith." Given these options, it is no wonder that theologians like John Milbank have argued that "Christian morality is a thing so strange, that it must be declared immoral or amoral according to all other human norms and codes of morality"—whether relativist or moralist.[5] One question for Evangelicals and Catholics is: How can we learn to be moral (and live with our ethical disagreements) without separating "faith and morals" in either of these ways?

I will not try directly to mediate pluralists and moralists, although I will periodically return to them as I take a different tack. It may initially sound like it makes the problem worse rather than better, but I will propose that Catholics and Evangelicals embed our moral and ethical agreements and disagreements in the context of other agreements and disagreements

4. Republication of the essay in note 3, with a new introductory paragraph in Robert N. Bellah, *Beyond Belief: Essays on Religion in a Post-Traditionalist World* (Berkeley: University of California Press, 1991) 168–89 (here 168).

5. John Milbank, "Can Morality be Christian?," *Studies in Christian Ethics* 10:2 (1997) 45–59 (here 45).

we have. This, I suggest, is how we will best learn to be ethical or moral, including being morally divided and having ethical disagreements.

Learning to Be Moral by Harvesting the Faith

Embedding our moral and ethical agreements and disagreements in our other agreements and disagreements is, of course, a challenge. There are numerous statements of Evangelical and Catholic agreements and disagreements, some from individuals or groups of individuals who speak only for themselves (like ECT or CCET) and some from groups officially sponsored by various churches. Even in cases where there has been official reception, it is not yet clear how such official reception relates to reception by particular churches in our cities and counties and countries. Nonetheless, the way I am going to work my way through these difficulties is by focusing on what Walter Cardinal Kasper, President of the Pontifical Council for Promoting Christian Unity, calls the Harvest Project. Kasper's Harvest Project, I suggest, provides one good way to articulate the context for our conversation about the morally divided body.[6]

Kasper moves between ecumenical optimists and pessimists—between those who see Christians inevitably moving toward the goal of visible unity and those discouraged by an "ecumenical winter" after forty years of spring and summer. Instead of such optimism or pessimism, Kasper takes up Paul's promise in Galatians 6:9: "For we will reap at harvest time, if we do not give up." The Project makes no claim to be an ecumenical promised land or to be occasion for rehashing all the traditional disagreements. It represents what Kasper calls some of those "intermediate steps" between the agreements we have and the visible unity toward which we hope, *sola gratia*, we are moving.[7] How?

6. Cardinal Walter Kasper, *Harvesting the Fruits: Basic Aspects of Christian Faith in Ecumenical Dialogue* (London: Continuum, 2009). The Harvest Project, as Kasper makes clear, is the product of Kasper and the staff of the Pontifical Council on Christian Unity.

7. *Harvesting the Fruits*, vi, 6, 8, 205, 206. I read the Harvest Project as an instance of the "new Symbolic theology" Kasper says is needed today—a theology (Kasper says) akin to that developed by J. A. Mohler at Tübingen on the Catholic side in the nineteenth century (*Harvesting*, 201), aimed at mediating between the great dogmatic theologies that have informed ecumenical consensus thus far and more modern or postmodern difficulties formulating binding doctrine. I think that the Harvest Project is also a step toward developing what Le Groupe des Dombes calls a way of receiving "a new corpus of doctrinal statements" in light of which to read earlier doctrinal conflicts; see Le Groupe des Dombes, *"One Teacher": Doctrinal Authority in the Church*, trans. Catherine

What Kasper harvests are the wheat and the chaff—the ecumenical consensus, convergences, and differences that remain in four dialogues on four key sets of issues. The four key dialogues are those of Catholics with Lutherans, Reformed, Anglicans, and Methodists. Some members of these communions have long claimed the label "Evangelical." But they are different from those Evangelicals who challenge Catholics by the way (as Thomas Rausch has put it) they can sometimes "represent 'streams' or 'movements' rather than clear ecclesial traditions."[8] This is one reason a comparison of ECT with the Harvest Project will be important.

But first let me briefly review the four key issues Kasper harvests: Jesus Christ and the Holy Trinity; salvation, justification, and sanctification; the Church; and the sacraments of baptism and Eucharist. My goal is not to survey all the agreements, convergences, and disagreements Kasper harvests. Instead, I will sketch just enough of its four key movements to set the context for consideration of the morally divided body.

First, there is consensus (Kasper points out) on the common Trinitarian and christological heritage. That is, the Holy Trinity is "the principle of communion," Father source of communion, Incarnate Word, Spirit Lord and Giver of life.[9] This will sound obvious to some, although (as Kasper points out) it is important to remember that this was the heritage shared in the sixteenth century but quickly eclipsed thereafter in arguments, polemics, and wars. Even with ongoing differences, the scripturally embedded Trinitarian and christological confessions set the context for most of these other differences rather than the reverse. How so?

Second, Kasper characterizes the key differences from the sixteenth century as disagreements over salvation, justification, and sanctification. The 1999 Lutheran-Catholic *Joint Declaration on the Doctrine of Justification*, also received by Methodist churches, articulates a consensus:

> In faith we together hold the conviction that justification is the work of the triune God. The Father sent his Son into the world to save sinners. The foundation and presupposition of justification

E. Clifford (Grand Rapids: Eerdmans, 2010 [French original 2005]) 127 (par. 410).

8. Thomas Rausch, "Catholics and Evangelical Relations: Signs of Progress," in Thomas P. Rausch, ed., *Catholics and Evangelicals: Do They Share a Common Future?* (Downers Grove, IL: InterVarsity, 2000) 37–55. For a brief survey of modern uses of "Evangelicals and Catholics" together, see James J. Buckley and David S. Yeago, "Introduction: A Catholic and Evangelical Theology?," in *Knowing the Triune God: The Work of the Spirit in the Practices of the Church* (Grand Rapids: Eerdmans, 2001) 1–20 (esp. 1–3).

9. *Harvesting the Fruits*, ch. 1.

is the incarnation, death, and resurrection of Christ. Justification thus means that Christ himself is our righteousness, in which we share through the Holy Spirit in accord with the will of the Father. Together we confess: By grace alone, in faith in Christ's saving work and not because of any merit on our part, we are accepted by God and receive the Holy Spirit, who renews our hearts while equipping and calling us to good works.[10]

Third, there are now what Kasper calls "common perspectives on the nature and mission of the Church"—its basis in the Trinitarian communion, the communion of saints at once "creature of the Word" and "sacrament of grace" and sacrament of the eschatological kingdom. It is these common perspectives that enable us to see more clearly why our division (as Vatican II puts it) "openly contradicts the will of Christ, scandalizes the world, and damages that most holy cause, the preaching of the Gospel to every creature."[11] In fact, it is this consensus on the communion of saints that drives the ecumenical venture—that enables us to see the wounds to the body of Christ that we are.

Fourth and finally, the stereotype of the Catholic Church of the sacraments and Protestant churches of the Word has been overcome. Kasper summarizes a consensus on baptism and (to a lesser extent) on the Eucharist. Baptism is incorporation into Christ and the gift of new life in Christ, and there is ordinarily mutual recognition of each other's baptisms. There is consensus (Kasper reports) on the central role of the Eucharist in expressing and deepening the Church's communion.[12]

Kasper, as I have said, not only summarizes the consensus on these four issues but also the convergences as well as differences or disagreements. I will not rehearse all these ongoing convergences or disagreements. The continuing divergences most relevant to our issues are those on salvation, justification, and sanctification. That is, Kasper contends that among the most significant work remaining to be done on the basis of this common confession is (quoting again the Joint Declaration) "*the relation between justification and social ethics.*" In Kasper's own words, we discover that "new questions—unknown to the Reformation—have emerged in the modern era, especially regarding *personal ethics* in questions of marriage and family,

10. *Harvesting the Fruits*, ch. 2 (136).

11. *Harvesting the Fruits*, ch. 3 (1 [quoting Vatican II's Decree on Ecumenism], 68, 69).

12. *Harvesting the Fruits*, ch. 4 (164, 190, 191)

human sexuality, and recent questions of bioethics"—along with "political and social ethics." In still other words, justification is "the starting point for the penetration of all worldly realities with the spirit of the Gospel," *including differences "that have recently emerged on ethical questions"—including "social, political, and environmental ethics."*

Here is the point of this harvest of agreements, convergences, and ongoing disagreements. Kasper's Harvest Project places our moral unities and divisions or ethical agreements and disagreements in the context of this consensus on Trinitarian and christological as well as ecclesiological and sacramental teaching. That is, he does not enter directly into the debate between the moral relativists and foundationalists I sketched above. Instead, he locates such agreements and convergences and disagreements in the context of a larger Catholic and Evangelical harvest. So the key first lesson is that we will learn to be moral or ethical by embedding these issues of personal, marital, familial, social, political, and environmental ethics in a Trinitarian and christological as well as ecclesiological and sacramental context. How?

Learning to be Ethical or Moral from ECT

Kasper is hopeful that "the consensus we have reached [on non-ethical issues] offers a solid basis for this clarification [on ethical issues]."[13] I do not know how Cardinal Kasper would recommend we proceed further in learning thus to be moral or ethical. I suggest we pose a different question. Kasper's Harvest Project does position us to ask not every question but one question about ECT: how does ECT fare in relation to Kasper's Harvest Project?

ECT has issued seven documents over the last fifteen years.[14] Until recently, the group proceeded under the leadership of Richard Neuhaus and Avery Cardinal Dulles on the Catholic side and Charles Colson and Timothy George on the Evangelical side. By my count there have been some seventy people who have signed the seven documents, although the most recent statement includes about a dozen Evangelicals and a dozen Catholics. I will measure ECT against Kasper's Harvest Project in three

13. *Harvesting the Fruits*, par. 20 (39).

14. I refer to these seven documents below. All these documents are posted on the *First Things* Web site, but the Web site does not give pages for the original texts as I will quote them below.

steps. First, I will say a word about the origins of ECT, relying on an account written by Fr. Neuhaus and Mr. Colson. Then I will describe a key challenge for the original ECT statement and how I got involved. Finally, I will summarize how the ECT statements contribute to our theme, before concluding with some challenges I think ECT must face to contribute further to the harvest.

Fr. Neuhaus and Mr. Colson have provided a brief history of the original ECT document.[15] Their account starts with a relationship between the two of them that began in 1984 as they discovered their common interest in "Christian engagement in the great cultural, social, and political tasks of our time"—but an engagement that they were convinced "would be largely futile, even counter-productive, unless that engagement was grounded in shared spiritual commitment and gospel truth."[16] At the same time, each of them was frequently approached by Evangelicals and Catholics who found one another "as Christians in various activities, notably in the pro-life movement and the charismatic renewal," as well as in prison ministries—Christians already involved together in some of "the great cultural, social, and political tasks of our time," hoping for Evangelicals and Catholics "to get together to explore what God might have in mind." And then there was what I will call a third strand: Evangelicals and Catholics "anguished by the growing conflicts between our communities in various parts of he world, especially in Latin America."

Indeed, it was this third strand that prompted the original ECT meetings in 1992. But it is important to keep in mind all three strands of the background: Neuhaus' and Colson's deep personal interests in what distinctively Christian engagements in the great cultural, social, and political questions of our time *might be*; attention to the fact that Evangelical and Catholic Christians *already find themselves so engaged* together but seek an articulation of their shared practices; and Christian *conflicts internationally* over Christian missions.

The initial ECT statement moves from what Catholics and Evangelicals share (summarized in the Apostles' Creed) to their hope for a common

15. Charles Colson and Richard John Neuhaus, "Introduction," in *Evangelicals and Catholics Together: Toward a Common Mission*, ed. Charles Colson and Richard John Neuhaus (Dallas: Word, 1995) ix–xiv. I have no doubt that others (particularly those, unlike myself, involved in the first statement) could and would add other perspectives to this story. I am simply relying on the written story that Colson and Neuhaus told in 1995 about a statement that was issued in 1992 and that arose from circumstances rooted in the mid-1980s.

16. Ibid., x–xi.

mission to the world.[17] But (the ECT argument goes) this common hope is blocked by a number of disagreements that are not mere "misunderstandings, misrepresentations, and caricatures"—disagreements over such issues as the Gospel and the Church and the individual Christian, apostolic succession and sacraments and ordinances, Mary and the saints.[18] How then to "contend together" or "struggle" against principalities and powers (Eph 6:12) in a common mission?

The statement does not aim to resolve all the disputes between Christians. Instead, in the context of the presiding responsibility to preach Christ's Gospel and sustain the church, the statement turns toward Christian "responsibility for the right ordering of civil society," noting that "[o]ur cooperation as citizens is animated by our convergence as Christians."[19] How? "Politics, law, and culture must be secured by moral truth." Thus, "only a virtuous people can be free and just, and that virtue is secured by religion," particularly religious freedom. The pattern of convergence among Catholics and Evangelicals "is, in large part, a result of common effort to protect human life, especially the lives of the most vulnerable among us." But there are also common contentions for (to give "a partial list") legal protection of the unborn, moral education in public education, against "the celebration of violence, sexual depravity, and antireligious bigotry in the entertainment industry," for a careful balancing of economics (including "a vibrant market economy") and politics and culture, a renewed appreciation of Western culture while engaging all cultures, "respect for the irreplaceable role of mediating structures in society—notably the family, churches, and myriad voluntary associations," and "a realistic and responsible understanding of America's part in world affairs." This is only "a partial list" and is not, we are assured, "a partisan 'religious agenda.'"

17. "Evangelicals and Catholics Together: The Christian Mission in the Third Millennium" (hereafter cited as "Christian Mission"), *First Things* 43 (1994) 15–22.

18. Ibid., 17–18.

19. Is it pressing matters too far to find here an analogy between Christian discipleship/citizenship and soul (animation)/body? Perhaps, although the analogy is explicit elsewhere (see below, "The Call to Holiness," 24b). William Cavanaugh has pointed out how the analogy between body/soul and politics/church is deadly in circumstances where the Church needs to be its own body of Christ in opposition to the body politic. William T. Cavanaugh, *Torture and Eucharist: Theology, Politics, and the Body of Christ* (Oxford: Blackwell, 1998) 58–70, 111–17, 157–65, 205–81.

Instead, these are elements of a common good "discussable on the basis of public reason."[20]

How can Christians (Catholics and Evangelical) contend for these public goods, given the combination of agreements and disagreements the statement previously sketched? The statement does not pretend to offer a complete answer to this question. Instead, it briefly sketches elements of what we might call a theology of conversion. "Christian witness is of necessity aimed at conversion," although it is not prudent "to proselytize among active adherents of another Christian community"—even though Evangelicals and Catholics disagree about the relationship between baptism and the experience of new birth in Christ.[21]

There are, it seems to me, a set of unresolved tensions here between affirmation of Christian agreement as well as disagreement—and affirmation of agreement on a relatively comprehensive religious, moral, and cultural agenda. These tensions create problems for learning how to be morally divided. The statement admits as much and promises future efforts to deal with unresolved issues.[22] But I think these unresolved tensions explain at least some of the critical responses to the original statement, with some Evangelicals disturbed by any doctrinal solidarity with Catholics and some Catholics certain that ECT is corrupted by a neoconservative political agenda.[23] The tensions certainly explain why, when I was invited to participate after the first statement, I hesitated—despite a dogmatic commitment (learned, I should say, from George Lindbeck and institutionalized by Carl Braaten and Robert Jenson in the Center for Catholic and Evangelical Theology) to any projects aimed at repairing the sins and wounds of Christian disunity.

Here is what I mean. Is the statement an affirmation of common ground (on the basis of "public reason") on a wide-ranging religious, moral, and cultural agenda—perhaps even more common ground on this agenda than we have on the apostolically biblical faith, given our traditional disagreements? Was a version of what I earlier called moralism or even

20. "Christian Mission," 18–20.

21. Ibid., 20–22.

22. Ibid., 22.

23. I do not aim here to survey the positive and negative responses online, in journals like *Christianity Today* and *First Things*, and in books and articles. For a recent analysis and bibliography, see Richard M. Rymarz, "Theological, Sociological and Historical Factors Influencing the Evangelical Turn in Contemporary Catholicism," *New Blackfriars* 91 (2010) 253–66.

American civil religion going to eclipse or perhaps even heal our traditional wounds? Time permitting, I think I could show that it is unfair to read the original ECT statement as thus grounding the Gospel in a version of American morality or civil religion. But it is a reading the document may well permit (without requiring) because the document emphasizes the contemporary moral and religious and cultural unanimities among some Christians, along with candid recognition of our traditional agreements and disagreements.

On the other hand, what did the statement have to offer Christians who were morally divided, who did not agree with ECT on issues ranging from abortion to euthanasia? Suppose that our own experiences or the most recent public opinion polls showed that Catholics and Evangelicals were as divided over these moral issues of life and death as other good Americans. What does the original ECT offer? Agreement on "public" goods, moral and religious values? But does this mean that our traditional agreements and disagreements are private reason, perhaps beyond reconciliation? How are our disagreements over these issues related to our traditional disagreements? In terms of my initial bifurcation between ethical pluralism and moralism, ECT might seem to err on the side of moralism. Again, time permitting, I think I could show that this too seems an unfair reading of the statement—although, once again, the statement may not say enough to protect itself against such a misreading.

After I was asked to join Evangelicals and Catholics Together, I had a frank conversation with Fr. Neuhaus about exactly these issues. Oversimplified, were the issues at stake primarily theological (Trinitarian and christological, ecclesiological and liturgical—as in what I would now call the Harvest Project)—or were they primarily religious, moral, and cultural? I had (and have) no objection to groups discussing and debating and pronouncing on any of the great social and political, religious and moral issues of life and death facing humanity in occasion-specific ways. But my own interests were more particular. Given the scandal and sin of Christian disunity, all of us must look for occasions where we are called to clarify, debate, and where possible resolve our disagreements on Trinitarian and christological as well as ecclesiological and liturgical issues. Absent that consensus (I thought then, and continue to think), there might be occasion-specific Catholic and Evangelical alignments on one or other issue (say, abortion or nuclear war), but I was skeptical of trying to harvest a more comprehensive civil or moral or religious consensus.

I remember how surprised Fr. Neuhaus was that I even asked the question about the theological priorities of ECT. He assured me that the issues were indeed primarily theological, not primarily in or over what I called American civil religion—that he did not envision the religious and moral and cultural agenda framing dogmatic claims but as occasion-specific application of Evangelical and Catholic truths. Was Fr. Neuhaus right? Was I right to believe him (as I did)? Let me take you through samples from the six subsequent statements so that I can draw some conclusions, and you can make up your own mind.

The second, third, and fourth ECT statements, it seems to me, essentially retrieve and expand on three theological paragraphs in the original statement on Christian Mission—and also parallel the first three issues in Kasper's Harvest Project. Thus, "The Gift of Salvation"[24]—published in January of 1998, before the Vatican's disappointing initial response to the *Joint Declaration* in June 1998 and the Lutheran-Catholic signing in October 1999—amplifies a paragraph in the original ECT statement confessing that "we are justified by grace through faith because of Christ."[25] The statement was necessary because this claim is central: unless Catholics and Evangelicals can agree on the essential doctrine that divided them in the sixteenth century, it makes little sense to think that their other agreements are anything but avoidance of those disagreements. The second ECT statement relocates the traditional Evangelical-Catholic debates over justification in the context of a central claim about "the gift of salvation." The results here very much parallel Kasper's Harvest Project: agreements, convergences, abiding disagreements now put in the context of the agreements and convergences.

The third ECT statement, "Your Word Is Truth,"[26] unpacks a paragraph in the original statement following on the insistence that "[t]he only unity to which we would give expression is unity in the truth"[27] and parallels the Harvest Project's summary about the primacy of Scripture within tradition. But this statement does this in its own way, reframing the traditional dispute over Scripture and tradition as a set of agreements and disagreements over Jesus' Johannine priestly prayer to "sanctify [the disciples] in truth; your

24. "The Gift of Salvation," *First Things* 79 (1998) 20–26.

25. "Christian Mission," 18.

26. "Your Word Is Truth," *First Things* 125 (2002) 38–42. See also Charles Colson and Richard John Neuhaus, eds., *Your Word Is Truth: A Project of Evangelicals and Catholics Together* (Grand Rapids: Eerdmans, 2002), which contains "Your Word Is Truth" and articles that led to the statement.

27. "Christian Mission," 18–19.

word is truth" (John 17:17). We affirm that the entire life of Christ's church "is to be held accountable to the final authority of Holy Scripture,"[28] even while affirming the "development of doctrine" in "the Apostles', Nicene, and Athanasian creeds, and in the conciliar resolution of disputes regarding the two natures of Christ and the triune life of God." Evangelicals recognize the need to address "the widespread misunderstanding" in (their) communities that *sola scriptura* means *nuda scriptura* (Scripture abstracted from its churchly context). Catholics in turn recognize the need to address the widespread misunderstanding in their community that Scripture and tradition are parallel and independent sources of authoritative teaching. Both Evangelicals and Catholics confess "the coinherence of Scripture and tradition" along with what they have to learn from each other's "devotional, disciplined, and prayerful engagement of Scripture"—even as they also admit ongoing disputes about the relationship between "the Holy Spirit, the Supreme Magisterium of God," "the entire community of the faithful" (*sensus fidelium*), the covenanted congregation of baptized believers, "wider synodical or episcopal connection," and the Petrine and other apostolic ministries.[29]

"The Communion of Saints," the fourth ECT statement,[30] once again unpacks a paragraph of the original ECT statement that Evangelicals and Catholics are "brothers and sisters in Christ"[31]—and parallels Kasper's move in the Harvest Project from salvation, justification, and sanctification to the Church, the "communion of saints" of the creeds. The Reformation disputes over justification not only came to eclipse an earlier consensus over apostolic faith; they also created a new set of disputes over the Church, its ministries, and its mission. ECT, following in the wake of Catholic-Orthodox and other Catholic-Evangelical dialogues, frames those disputes with a theology of the communion of saints. Isaiah's thrice-holy God is the Trinitarian communion into which all "human beings are called to participate."[32] This participation is "necessarily communal"—to listen to the word of God, to pray to God for each other, to study the Bible, to evangelize with rather than against one another, "give ourselves in service to the poor and needy" (even while "individuals may disagree about what constitutes a just social

28. "Your Word Is Truth," 39b.

29. Ibid., 40a.

30. "The Communion of Saints," *First Things* 131 (2003) 26–33.

31. "Christian Mission," 18.

32. "The Communion of Saints," 28.

order"). The communion of saints is also our communion in "sacraments or ordinances," although the Evangelical-Catholic "inability to be one at the table of the Lord in Holy Communion" is communion at its "most manifestly and painfully imperfect." Finally, noting that the most common use of "communion of saints" in the early Church was "the enduring bond between the faithful on earth and the faithful who had gone before" (especially the martyrs), the statement notes a number of disagreements within this communion of the living and the dead—including disagreements over prayers to the saints and purgatory.

So far, although any of us may quarrel with these statements on a number of grounds, it can hardly be said that any cultural, moral, or religious agenda has dominated ETC's theological (Trinitarian, christological, and ecclesiological) agenda. It is ECT's fifth and sixth statements that anticipate the Harvest Project's extension of the harvest to what Kasper (and this conference) calls moral division and ethical disagreement among Christians—although the ECT statements privilege neither "ethics" nor "morality" as a way to measure these divisions and disagreements. Instead, "The Call to Holiness," the fifth statement,[33] moves from Church as communion of saints "to consider the ways in which our communities and their individual members can and must foster and embody holiness." The triune God calls the Church to be a holy people. This transformation is experienced in different ways by different people but focused on the inseparability of faith and baptism. Christians only too often fail to measure up to these standards, and there must be "a continuing call to repentance and transformation of life," a continuing call to become who we are. This includes "obedience to the moral law permanently inscribed by the Creator in human nature (Romans 2:15)," the moral precepts of the Decalogue, especially Christ's commandment of love. While individual Christians have different vocations, all are called to prayerful study of Scripture, corporate worship on the Lord's Day, and "confession of our sins and failures to God and one another." Our mission to the world is "evangelization in the broadest sense"—that is, "proclaiming the good news of Jesus Christ to all people and bringing that gospel to bear, by word and deed, on the totality of things." The call to holiness is not only occasion-specific but (and here I use a lexicon not used by ECT) occasion-comprehensive, bearing on the "the totality of things."[34] Christians are called to do this in different ways—by

33. "The Call to Holiness," *First Things* 151 (2005) 23–26.

34. William A. Christian Sr., *Doctrines of Religious Communities. A Philosophical*

being missionaries to other lands, to parents and families, businessmen and women, and politicians. Here is where the fifth ECT statement begins most clearly reintegrating with the first statement, for holiness of life "requires us to exemplify and advance a culture of life. This includes a defense of religious freedom and the marriage-based family, resistance to evils such as abortion, euthanasia, eugenics, and coercive population control, and a devotion to justice for all, especially for the poor." Christians can expect "opposition and setbacks" in their efforts to live a life of holiness, borne with patience and joy in Christ as "indivisible aspects of the Holy Spirit's work in our day."

The question becomes how to thus reach out, how to be thus occasion-comprehensive. "That They May Have Life," [35] the sixth statement, continues the movement into what is ordinarily called "morality" or "ethics." The statement has two purposes. "Our primary purpose," the authors state (and it important that this is "primary"), "is to explain to our communities why we believe that support for a culture of life is an integral part of Christian faith and therefore a morally unavoidable imperative of Christian discipleship." But they also "intend, however briefly and inadequately, to make a case for what is commonly called 'a culture of life'—and to do so in a way that invites public deliberation and engages questions of public policy." On this second score, they aim "to move beyond 'culture wars' to a reasonable deliberation of the right ordering of our life together," a new humanism. More concretely, the statement focuses on "a commitment to a culture of life, which includes the protection and care of the unborn, the severely disabled, the dependent elderly, and the dying," as well as "the poor, the marginalized, and those who, for whatever reason, are vulnerable to neglect or exploitation of others."[36]

Study (New Haven: Yale University Press, 1987), chs. 7 and 8 (esp. 225–27). Christian distinguishes doctrinal topic-comprehensiveness (a community has doctrines on every topic, on everything morally or ethically true or right, without limits), occasion-comprehensiveness (a community has doctrines bearing on any occasion of human activity, without claiming to teach what is true and right about everything about that occasion), occasion-specificness (a community has teachings about specific occasions of human activity). I will use these distinctions later. I tend to think that the Catholic drive toward occasion-comprehensiveness risks topic-comprehensiveness (not acknowledging its limits), while an Evangelical drive toward occasion-specificity may create a morally nimble community, aware of its limits, but more subject to moral diffusion.

35. "That They May Have Life," *First Things* 166 (2006) 18–25.

36. Ibid., 18a–20b. Note that, in contrast to the first ECT statement, the case for a culture of life is briefer than the case for integrating the culture of life into Christian faith

How, then, to speak with these aims to these audiences, with these priorities? "The culture of life"—here ECT clearly echoes, without specifically referring to, John Paul II's 1995 encyclical *Evangelium Vitae*—"is made possible and imperative by the gospel of life." This gospel "is centered in Jesus Christ"—his life and death and resurrection and promised return. But this gospel also includes the larger biblical story of creation (including the creation of male and female in God's image), sin typified in the story of the first murderer (Cain), the restoration of humanity in Christ, the confrontation of Christians with ancient and modern sin and evil until the end time. This "gospel of life" is the context for "a culture of life" centered on love of neighbor. But ECT is here specific. We focus on the Decalogue's mandate not to kill as "the most basic commandment of neighbor-love," "the negatively stated minimum of what we owe to our fellow human beings." The statement moves (once again, very much like John Paul II's *Evangelium Vitae*) from a brief application of the seventh commandment to unjust aggressors (self-defense, just wars, capital punishment) to its application to the innocent (abortion, euthanasia, experimentation with embryos).[37]

Some Catholics and Evangelicals as well as ethical and moral relativists and absolutists might have thought that the next logical move would have been for ECT to develop more detailed statements on these issues. This would have required more engagement on moral and ethical issues on the grounds of our agreements on Jesus and the triune God, Church and worship—and more apologetical engagement with what I earlier called moral relativists and absolutists in our and other cultures, relativists worried that Christians are out to impose their views of moral absolutism or American civil religion on them, moral absolutists attentive to how ECT would respond to ethical pluralists or those with competing absolutes. That is, ECT could have continued the movement of shaping a culture of life with the Gospel of life, delving more deeply into agreements and disagreements on the response that Gospel requires of us in the face of attacks on innocent life from birth to death. Or we could have expanded outward into the litany of evils cited in the sixth statement: "genocide, unjust war, innocent victims of just wars, economic exploitation, the neglect and abuse of children, the disrespect and mistreatment of women, the abandonment of the aged, racial oppression and discrimination, the persecution of religious

(the Gospel of life)—and distances itself from co-belligerency and the culture wars in favor of a more irenic new humanism.

37. "That They May Have Life," 20a–21b.

believers, and religious and ideological fanaticisms that are the declared enemies of freedom."[38]

Instead, ECT's seventh and most recent statement moved to—Mary.[39] Why? Speaking for myself (and that is what I do throughout this paper) and not for ECT or even the Catholics in ECT, the reason is important. What is the context of our ethical or moral agreements and disagreements? It is (to review what I have written so far) our biblically shaped Nicene confession, the gift of salvation, and the communion of saints—holiness of life, living the Gospel of life by living a culture of life. But the more we extend agreements (always with ongoing disagreements) toward particular issues of the gospel and culture of life, the more it is important to keep in mind our agreements as well as our disagreements. What then about our agreements and disagreements over one specific example of holiness of life, Mary—mentioned in the first ECT Statement.[40] The statement on Mary is, in fact, a key piece of evidence for the thesis emerging here: that ECT, far from letting our moral/ethical agreements/disagreements set the agenda, has worked at reintegrating those agreements and disagreements into our agreements and disagreements over the triune God, the incarnate Word, the Spirit giver of life to the communion of saints.

Thus, "Do Whatever He Tells You," the seventh ECT statement, aims "to examine anew, as Evangelicals and Catholics together, the place of Mary in Christian faith and life," addressing but not resolving "all the familiar differences on this subject." The examination takes places through reflection on Scripture, including "the typological reading of Mary, and of Christ, in the Old Testament. Mary is "full of grace" and "blessed," virgin and mother, *theotokos* and handmaid and disciple, participant in Jesus' suffering and gathered with the disciples on Pentecost.[41]

However, most of the document is devoted to each side addressing a word to the other about the abiding differences—"A Catholic Word to Evangelicals,"[42] and the twice as long "An Evangelical Word to Catholics."[43] Catholics unpack "four aspects" of Catholic teaching: Mary's perpetual

38. Ibid., 21a.

39. "Do Whatever He Tells You: The Blessed Virgin Mary in Christian Faith and Life," *First Things* 197 (2009) 49–58.

40. "Christian Mission," xi.

41. "Do Whatever He Tells You," 49b–51a.

42. Ibid., 51a–53b.

43. Ibid., 53b–58b.

virginity, Immaculate Conception, bodily Assumption, and her role in the communion of saints. The Evangelicals lament "the neglect of Mary in Evangelical theology and hope for its recovery," beginning with the thoughts of Luther and Calvin on Mary. They respond to the four teachings. While affirming the virgin birth, they find the Catholic teaching on Mary's perpetual virginity "adiaphorous teaching, neither required nor forbidden." While affirming "much of what this teaching [Mary's Immaculate Conception] is intended to convey," they do not accept the sinlessness of Mary because of Scripture and tradition. Although the doctrine of Mary's assumption "presupposes a number of things that are indeed a part of our common Christian confession," there is no biblical warrant for the assumption, and the ambiguity of Catholic teaching on whether Mary actually died (an ambiguity admittedly present in Christian apocryphal writings) creates still other difficulties for the doctrine. Finally, while affirming their honor and love and praise of Mary, they do not think that such beliefs and attitudes lead to "her invocation, intercession, or mediation." "We both want to avoid Marian excess on the one hand and Marian narrow-mindedness on the other, but we continue to differ on what is excessive and what is too restrictive."

My point is not to analyze fully, much less evaluate, this most recent statement—or, for that matter, the other statements. The point, for purposes of thinking about the morally divided body, is that these Evangelicals and Catholics agree that Mary is a model of holiness—and therefore "a model and encouragement in our efforts to advance the culture of life."[44] Moral unity or disunity, ethical agreement or disagreement abstracted from the Catholic and Evangelical harvest may serve a variety of causes. It will not serve a Catholic and Evangelical one.

Some Tentative Conclusions

How can Catholics and Evangelicals learn to be moral or ethical (and how to handle divisions and disagreements)? Even more (I think) than Kasper's Harvest Project, ECT has integrated our moral and ethical disputes into our other agreements and disagreements—the consensus over Scripture and the Nicene faith, the consensus over justification and the gift of salvation, the consensus over the communion of saints, and over baptism. Without this integration with this emerging harvest of Catholic and Evangelical

44. Ibid., 58a.

faith, our agreements and disagreements will remain bound to the terms of our culture, whether we are moralists or morally pluralists. I think ECT shows one way to learn to be morally or ethically united or divided, or to resist being merely ethical or moral. My argument has been text-based and, I think, could be shown wrong quite easily—by showing that I have misread the ECT documents in some way.

Insofar as I am correct, can this ecumenical venture be sustained? We shall see. The deaths of Avery Cardinal Dulles (December 12, 2008) and Fr. Neuhaus (January 8, 2009) were a huge loss. Mr. George Weigel and Mr. Charles Colson are now co-executive directors of ECT, while Dean Timothy George and Fr. Thomas Guarino are lead theologians. At our first post-Dulles/Neuhaus meeting this past fall, we decided next to take up the topic of "religious freedom"—a topic mentioned in the original ECT statement[45] as well as a topic of wide-ranging historical and philosophical and political importance. A meeting on the topic, which I could not attend, took place last weekend. Will ECT issue a document that teaches us how to be "religiously free" and resists the temptation to be merely "religious," as it has so far shown how to be ethical or moral, and resist the temptation to be merely moral or ethical? We shall see.

In the meanwhile, let me raise three questions that will be important for future harvests on our moral and ethical agreements and disagreements.

1. How occasion-specific shall we be, and how to be occasion-specific, for the sake of visible unity? In a forthcoming article in *The Journal of Ecumenical Studies*, Mike Root has shown in much more detail than Kasper's Harvest Project that ethics is not a new theme in ecumenical discussions. But Root also shows that the dialogues have thus far focused on "values, perspectives, visions" more than on "specific rules and practices."[46] Root's article is very persuasive. But how specific do we have to be, and how shall we be specific? In focusing one of its statements on issues of life and the taking of life, ECT has tried to provide at least some "specific rules and practices" while embedding those rules and practices in the larger "values, perspectives, visions" of its statements on God and Christ, salvation and justification, church and holiness. But how much more specific would we have to be about birth and death for visible unity? Christian discipleship *coram Deo*

---

45. "Christian Mission," xxiii.

46. Michael Root, "Ethics in Ecumenical Dialogues: A Survey and Analysis," *Journal of Ecumenical Studies* 45:3 (2010) 357–375, and ch. 8 below.

involves individuals and communities in particular physical, social, and historical circumstances. We are complex bundles of embodied emotions, passions, feelings, thoughts, and beliefs enacted in these complex physical, social, and historical circumstances. So addressing a moral or ethical issue on any specific occasion is complex, ranging from consensus on Paul's gifts of the Holy Spirit through the development of the monastic life and other practices to specific legal and political policies. What are the specific moral and ethical issues on which we must agree for visible unity? Consideration of each of the Ten Commandments might be a starting point.

2. How occasion-comprehensive shall we be, and how to be occasion-comprehensive, for the sake of visible unity? This question naturally leads to another: how comprehensive do our agreements have to be? Kasper's Harvest Project mentions personal as well as social ethics, marriage and familial ethics, social and political, bio- and environmental ethics. How comprehensive shall we be, while acknowledging that there are limits to what a Catholic and Evangelical community can and should teach about anything, including matters ethical and moral? This sort of question will lead us (I think) to take up issues like those John Paul II takes up in *Veritatis Splendor*, his 1993 encyclical on "The Splendor of Truth." Here the late Petrine minister points out that traditional moral teaching covers "the many spheres of human life [*varios et dissimiles vitae humanae ambitus*]" (paragraph 4). Today, faced by a crisis within the Christian community separating freedom and truth, John Paul says, it is "necessary to reflect on the whole of the Church's moral teaching [*de institutionis moralis Ecclesiae universitate*]." In my lexicon, we are driven not only to deal with a variety of specific occasions (the many spheres of human life) but also more comprehensively (the whole of the Church's moral teaching). Here is where I would locate what seems to me to be one of the unsolved issues in ECT: how shall our comprehensive posture toward the world include (on the one hand) both contention against principalities and powers[47] and co-belligerency[48]—and (on an other hand) "public reason"[49] or a new humanism of "reasonable deliberation of the right

47. "Christian Mission," xxii–xxviii.
48. "The Communion of Saints," 27b.
49. "Christian Mission," 20.

ordering of our life together"?[50] For Catholics, these are what a recent book by (and on) Alasdair MacIntyre calls "intractable disputes about the natural law," even among Catholics—including debates over the nature and aims of "ethics" and/or "morality."[51]

3. Finally and above all, we must be able to show the God-difference that our ethical and moral disagreements make. I do not primarily mean our talk *about* God, important as that is. I mean our talk *before and to* God, our prayer, our liturgical life as a whole and in its details, Word and sacrament. The God to whom we pray is rightly identified in the Harvest Project and ECT as, of course, the God of Scripture and the Nicene faith, gathering a communion of saints for the end time. And praying to this God must be central to Catholic and Evangelical discussion and debate—and it is certainly central for the members of ECT. The ECT gap on this score is not a question of personal praying but corporate praying—and not so much the corporate praying of baptism but of Eucharist. As you may recall, ECT's statement on the Communion of Saints (2006) agreed that Evangelical-Catholic "inability to be one at the table of the Lord in Communion" is communion at its "most manifestly and painfully imperfect."[52] If ECT is ahead of Kasper's formidable Harvest Project on a couple of matters of "ethics and morality," we are behind on matters of Eucharist and ministry. I think it would be helpful for us to tackle the issue of eucharistic practice and ethical/moral doctrine. I do not say this in a

---

50. "That They May Have Life," 19.

51. Lawrence S. Cunningham, ed., *Intractable Disputes about the Natural Law: Alasdair MacIntyre and Critics* (Notre Dame: University of Notre Dame Press, 2009), including MacIntyre's dispute with Cardinals Kasper and (then) Cardinal Ratzinger over philosophical and theological reason(s). Here, also, is where Evangelical and Catholic discussion can join in the name-calling culture wars between moralists and moral pluralists. Academic philosophers also disagree on what ethics or morality is, or are. To deal with these disagreements, contemporary philosophers sometimes distinguish between "morality" and "ethics," distinguishing those who (like, in different and opposed ways, Kant or the utilitarians) give a priority to questions like "What is obligatory to do?" and those who (like, in different and opposed ways, Aristotle or Nietzsche) give priority to broader questions like "What is the good or worthwhile life to live?" See, for example, Charles Taylor, "Modern Moral Rationalism," in *Weakening Philosophy: Essays in Honor of Gianni Vattimo*, ed. Santiago Zabala (Montreal: McGill-Queen's University Press, 2007) 57–76. And these disagreements lead to disagreements over the relationship between "the moral sense" and "the religious sense" (*Splendor Veritatis* §98).

52. "The Communion of Saints," 30.

triumphalistic spirit, as if Catholics and Evangelicals who practice the Eucharist on a liturgical calendar had all the truth and Evangelicals and Catholics who do not are the beggars—as if the gift-exchange will be one-sided. Unless we bind Eucharist and ethics, we will not grip the interaction of the Synoptic and Johannine suppers, where eating the bread and washing each other's feet are necessary complements and challenges to each other. It can hardly be said that churches that regularly practice the Eucharist have embodied the essential biblical bond of eucharistic worship and ethics. Catholics need Evangelical help on this issue, as on other issues. More importantly, our eucharistic prayer and practice is who we are before the triune God. If we are not visibly unified here, we will not be unified morally and ethically. If we are divided here, we are divided morally and ethically as well.

8

Ethics in Ecumenical Dialogues: A Survey and Analysis[1]

Michael Root

Two perceptions dominate discussions of the topic of this essay: "Ethics in Ecumenical Dialogues." On the one hand, it is widely said that the need for an ecumenical discussion of ethics and ethical questions is ever more important, both because of the need for the church to give a common moral witness and because of the appearance of new, potentially church-dividing or communion-hindering ethical disputes between and within the churches.[2] On the other hand, laments are common that ecumenical dialogues, mired down in arguments over classical dogmatic differences, have generally failed to take up ethical matters.[3]

The first perception is all too accurate. The churches certainly do need to give a common moral witness. The 2008 American presidential election demonstrated the divisive potential of differences between churches over ethics. Many of us, myself included, have been pulled into difficult conversations about the continuing unity (or lack thereof) of our denominations

1. This essay began as an oral presentation and retains much of the style appropriate to such a presentation. It was originally published in the *Journal of Ecumenical Studies* (45:3), copyright 2010, and is used here with permission.

2. I prefer the term "communion-hindering" as more ecclesiologically accurate, but will use the more widely accepted phrase "church-dividing."

3. I will use the terms "ethical" and "moral" interchangeably in this essay.

as they are ripped apart by disagreements on sexual ethics. The second perception, however—that ecumenical dialogues have neglected ethical matters—is less accurate. As the list of dialogues that have addressed ethical matters shows (see appendices), a wide range of dialogues have taken up the nature of Christian ethics, the place of ethics in the unity of the church, and specific moral questions, and they have done so steadily since the 1960s. The literature is far more extensive than I anticipated. The list is, I will grant, somewhat misleading in that many dialogues have taken up ethical matters only in passing. Nevertheless, we should remember that when the current wave of ecumenical dialogues began to gain momentum in the 1960s, ethical differences were rarely seen as church-dividing. We should not be surprised that dialogues have given more attention to such matters as baptism, Eucharist, and ministry, whose role in division is manifest, than to ethical questions, whose divisive potential is only now becoming evident.

In this essay, I will survey and briefly analyze the discussions of ethics in ecumenical dialogues. To do so in a text of this length means that I must often handle matters quickly that deserve greater attention and will not be able to present the full range of supporting citations. Much of the presentation will be simply descriptive, which I hope will be more informative than boring. I will end with some comments on the general question of differences over ethics as church-dividing matters.

I must first, however, delimit the topic. Defining "ethics" is an elusive task. Is the distinct field of "ethics" a modern invention, perhaps bound up with unique aspects of modernity?[4] Even if that is true, some distinction between "fides et mores" is ancient in the church, and the distinction between the ceremonial, the governmental, and the moral law of the Old Testament was important for the early church's appropriation of the Hebrew Scriptures.[5] I will make a commonsense (but utterly circular) discrimination that ethical matters are those where judgments of ethical right or wrong or ethical obligation are paramount. Ethical matters cannot be strictly separated from others, however. In ecumenical discussions of divorce and remarriage, the ethical and sacramental are inextricably intertwined. In this essay, I will focus only on the ethical side of such questions.

---

4. See, e.g., Arne Rasmusson, "Ecclesiology and Ethics: The Difficulties of Ecclesial Moral Reflection," *Ecumenical Review* 52 (2000) 180–94.

5. Jaroslav Pelikan, *The Emergence of the Catholic Tradition (100–600)* (Chicago: University of Chicago Press, 1971) 16–18.

A decision must also be made about the other half of my title: "Ecumenical Dialogues." I will focus only on official dialogues between the churches and thus will not discuss the group Evangelicals and Catholics Together, admittedly an important example of dialogue on ethical questions, nor the work of such others as the Groupe des Dombes. I will take up multilateral dialogues (e.g., by the Faith and Order Commission of the National Council of Churches) when these have the character of a dialogue, that is, an encounter of the churches on an ethical question. I will not take up the Justice, Peace and the Integrity of Creation process or the Ecclesiology and Ethics project of the World Council of Churches, which seem to me not to have been an encounter of the churches in the quite the same way. The official dialogues provide us more than enough to work with. I cannot promise that I have found all such dialogues. I know of, but have not been able to find a copy of, a dialogue on marriage (in the context of addressing mixed marriages) from Australia. A few Canadian and French dialogues may also be missing.

I will first look at discussions in the dialogues about ethics and the place of ethics in the churches, and then turn to discussions of specific moral questions.

Dialogues That Deal with Ethics in General[6]

The Importance or Necessity of a Common Moral Witness and/or Engagement

Perhaps the most common ethical element in ecumenical dialogues is an affirmation of the importance of a common moral witness by the churches. They often begin with an affirmation of the unity of faith and life: for example, the US Catholic-Reformed dialogue stated: "We acknowledge that belief and behavior, faith and works, should not be separated. Therefore issues of ethics and morality, which involve the relation between conscience and authority, are not peripheral to but at the heart of the faithful hearing of the Gospel."[7] If ethics is central in this way, then the churches need to

---

6. All ecumenical texts will be referred to by the abbreviation found in Appendix 1. Many can be found in multiple locations. When possible, I will refer to paragraph numbers, so that those using a different published version can locate the citation. When a dialogue does not have paragraph numbers, I can only refer to the page number of the version given in Appendix 1.

7. C-R USA 1985, ¶42.

pursue what the WCC-Vatican Joint Working Group referred to as "that unity in moral life which is Christ's will."[8] Often, this needed engagement is described in terms of an engagement for social justice. As the (European) Leuenberg Church Fellowship (Lutheran, Reformed, United) put it: "Christians have been commissioned to take a stance, in warning and admonition, everywhere where human dignity, human life and the integrity of creation is being infringed upon and violated."[9]

Dialogue language is not completely uniform on this matter. The Catholic-Evangelical dialogue on mission (1984) noted a difference of opinion between Catholics and some Evangelicals over the degree to which the church as a body should take up such engagement (in distinction from individual Christians).[10] In addition, the issues lifted up for common witness vary. Unlike others, the just named Catholic-Evangelical dialogue mentioned the need for a "united witness" that could "testify to the sanctity of sex, marriage, and family life; agitate for the reform of permissive abortion legislation . . . [and] promote Christian moral values in public life and in the education of children."[11] I would guess that not all dialogues would agree on that list.

If such a common ethical witness is called for, is failure to manifest such a witness a sign or even cause of division? The language of the dialogues would suggest such. The Catholic-Reformed international dialogue stated in relation to witness in the area of Justice, Integrity, and the Integrity of Creation: "The most profound convictions of their faith oblige both churches to render decisive witness in these fields. They would imperil the integrity of their teaching if they failed to give it."[12] If the "integrity of teaching" is at stake, then failure would seem to be at least potentially church-dividing. The international Lutheran-Reformed dialogue addressed this question directly. After affirming a legitimate diversity in ethics, it stated: "But here too diversity can become illegitimate; there are certain ethical beliefs which cease to express the agreement reached on the understanding of the gospel. This obstructs the path leading to the common table of the Lord and thereby breaks church fellowship. . . . It is therefore important that, both within our churches and communities, as well as between our

8. JWG 1998: I,4; 32.
9. Leuenberg 1995, 113.
10. C-Evan Int 1984, 411.
11. Ibid., 433.
12. C-R Int 1990, ¶159.

churches, we engage in a common search for common witness and service where the important issues of our day are concerned (peace, justice, race, gender, bioethics, etc.)." Diversity "does not imply undifferentiated acceptance of any or all attitudes or opinions."[13] The suspension of southern African churches from membership in the Lutheran World Federation and the World Alliance of Reformed Churches is explicitly cited as an example of such illegitimate ethical diversity.

The Most Comprehensive Discussion of Ethics in an Ecumenical Dialogue

But when is an ethical difference church-dividing? The dialogue that has most directly addressed that question is also the dialogue that has dealt most comprehensively with ethical questions: the 1994 Anglican-Roman Catholic International Commission (ARCIC) report titled *Life in Christ: Morals, Communion and the Church*. The previous ARCIC report, *Church as Communion* (1991), had already said, in the context of listing of elements of communion that bind the churches together: "Also constitutive of life in communion is acceptance of the same basic moral values, the sharing of the same vision of humanity created in the image of God and recreated in Christ, and the common confession of the one hope in the final consummation of the Kingdom of God."[14]

Life in Christ uses the same language of a common set of "basic moral values." In its first paragraph, it claims that the churches share a "common perspective" and acknowledge the "same underlying values." Later, it outlines four basic moral questions and states: "At this fundamental level of inquiry and concern, we believe, our two Communions share a common vision and understanding."[15] It then discusses specific differences (on divorce and contraception) against the background of this shared moral vision. Because of the agreement on shared moral values, the more detailed differences on specific practices and rule are bearable. Differences are "on the level of derived conclusions rather than fundamental values."[16] Or, in the context of a very brief discussion of abortion and homosexuality, it is claimed that differences are not at the level of "fundamental moral values,"

13. L-R Int 1989, ¶72.
14. ARCIC 1991, ¶45.
15. ARCIC 1994, ¶11.
16. Ibid., ¶83.

but of their "implementation."[17] Thus: "In the course of history Anglicans and Roman Catholics have disagreed on certain specific matters of moral teaching and practice, but they continue to hold to the same vision of human nature and destiny fulfilled in Christ."[18] The claim is explicitly made that the existing differences are not church-dividing.[19]

The ARCIC argument is a particular form of what Harding Meyer has labeled an internally differentiated consensus.[20] Internal to a particular question (e.g., marriage and divorce), one distinguishes between the consensus needed for communion (here, agreement on "basic moral values") and permitted diversity (in implementation or on more specific matters of teaching and practice). As we will see, some such appeal to a differentiated consensus is common in dialogues on ethics, as in other dialogues (it is hard to avoid such arguments—Meyer's term is essentially a useful description of what one almost inevitably seeks). What is specific to the ARCIC argument—and what is, I believe, its weakness—is its privileging of the general over the particular. The dialogue seeks agreement at a level (the dialogue's term) of generality, that is, in values, visions, and perspectives. These values, visions, and perspectives allow diversity at the more particular and concrete level of specific rules and practices. At this point, I will simply note this characteristic; I will come back to it at the end of the essay. In the meantime, I can only note that *Life in Christ* is the only dialogue systematically to present a detailed argument about why a set of ethical disagreements need not be church-dividing. Other dialogues make such claims, but without argumentation, relying on the reader's intuition that the dialogue has the matter right.

17. Ibid., ¶84.

18. Ibid., ¶96.

19. Ibid., ¶1.

20. For his more complete statement in English, see Harding Meyer, "Ecumenical Consensus: Our Quest for and the Emerging Structures of Consensus," *Gregorianum* 77 (1996) 213–25. A slightly more developed position is found in Harding Meyer, "Die Prägung einer Formel: Ursprung und Intention," in *Einheit—Aber Wie? Zur Tragfähigkeit der ökumenischen Formel vom "differenzierten Konsens,"* ed. Harald Wagner (Freiburg: Herder, 2000) 36–58.

Other General Ethical Questions in Ecumenical Dialogues

Ethical Methods

Other more general ethical matters are addressed in dialogues. With varying degrees of self-consciousness, some dialogues have addressed questions of ethical theory or method: for example, natural law versus divine command ethics. Sometimes the dialogue partners agree on ethical method; in a few cases, differences are noted.

The most common ethical method or theory present in the dialogues might be generally described as a natural-law-as-illuminated-by-revelation approach. The US Catholic-Reformed dialogue referred to a universal moral law known by reason and revelation, inscribed in the human heart.[21] This approach often appeals to a grounding in creation. Pope John Paul II and Ecumenical Patriarch Bartholomew I stated: "It is on the basis of our recognition that the world is created by God that we can discern an objective moral order within which to articulate a code of environmental ethics."[22]

Other ethical approaches can be found in the dialogues. Some appeal to communion as generative of an ethical perspective (e.g., the US Anglican-Catholic dialogue: "Upon the corporate or social character of the Trinity's redemptive action for the whole human family the morality of the Christian community is built"[23]). Some dialogues orient ethics more eschatologically; the Christian life is to find forms that anticipate the justice and peace of God's reign (e.g, the US Anglican-Lutheran statement on *Implications of the Gospel*, A-L USA 1988: §114, or the US Catholic-Reformed dialogue, C-R USA 1985: 426). In one case, it is said that the Bible constitutes "a yardstick for Christian faith and life."[24]

Rarely are such questions of ethical theory or method seen as matters of serious dispute. Differences are sometimes noted, however, as in the international Catholic-Evangelical dialogue (C-Evan 1985: §78) and the international Lutheran-Methodist dialogue (L-Meth Int 1984: §75).

I have found only two cases where different approaches to ethics have been extensively explored in dialogues. First, the Lutheran-Adventist dialogue discussed differing attitudes toward the Ten Commandments and "law" more generally as background for their differing attitudes toward

21. C-R USA 1980, 420.

22. C-O Rm-Cnstnpl 2002, 184f.

23. A-C USA 1977, 169.

24. AIC-R Int 1999, Opening Affirmations.

Sabbath. While they seemed to see the general difference over law as merely reflecting different emphases, the question of Sabbath practice was more difficult, though not equally for both parties. While Lutherans said they could "respect" Adventist Sabbath practice, the Adventists still said that they found Sabbath "an essential part of divine design in Creation." Whether Lutherans meet the Adventist standard of Sabbath practice is not said.[25] What might appear as mere difference at a general level ends up being embodied in a disagreement over a specific practice.

Second, a more extended discussion across more than one dialogue occurred in relation to a perceived Lutheran-Reformed difference in political ethics, summarized as a perceived opposition of the ethical catchwords "Two Kingdoms Doctrine" (Lutheran) and "Lordship of Christ" (Reformed). A US Lutheran-Reformed dialogue addressed the question in the mid-1960s. It did not claim "complete agreement" but did believe they had "moved together" on the question.[26] Fifteen years later, the topic was taken up by two subgroups within the Leuenberg Church Fellowship, whose results were included in the 1981 Driebergen Report. Both groups argued that the two positions are not mutually exclusive. In fact, each position includes elements of the other, and neither was entirely specific to one confession or the other.[27] While the two outlooks cannot be entirely harmonized, they are "critically complementary" in the sense that each tends to guard against dangers inherent in the other.[28] Since the Leuenberg churches were already in altar and pulpit fellowship, they were already committed to the non-church-dividing character of this difference. In 1993, a new round of US Lutheran-Reformed conversations affirmed the results of the Driebergen Report.[29]

Differing ethical theories or methods thus have not created obstacles to ecumenical rapprochement, except, as in the case of the Adventist-Lutheran dialogue, when they are connected with a problematic divergence in practice.

---

25. Ad-L Int 2000, 11f.

26. L-R USA 1966, 152, 177.

27. Leuenberg 1982, 40, 45.

28. Leuenberg 1982, 41–43, 50.

29. L-R 1993, 59–61.

Ethics and Ecclesial Authority

Various Catholic-Protestant (including Anglican) dialogues have addressed, though not in detail, a final general question in relation to ethics, viz., the authority of the church's ethical teachings. The international Catholic-Methodist dialogue found a "point of divergence" around the question: "What persons or bodies in the Church can give guidance on moral issues and with what authority? . . . In both our Churches we are under ecclesiastical authority, but we recognize a difference in that some pronouncements of the Catholic Church are seen as requiring a higher degree of conscientious assent from Catholics than the majority of pronouncements of the responsible bodies of Methodism require of Methodists."[30]

A problem is created for dialogues, since they often must compare an extensive body of ethical and social magisterial teaching from the Catholic Church with less binding and more various statements from the non-Catholic body (commented on both by L-C Int 1994: §276 and ARCIC 1994: §101). As the WCC-Vatican Joint Working Group stated, there can be "an imbalance and lack of realism in the dialogue if one easily compares the official teachings of some churches with the more diffuse estimates of the general belief and practice of others."[31]

More fundamentally, the difference touches the freedom of conscience of the individual Christian in relation to the responsibility of the church to form that conscience. In *Life in Christ*, the Anglicans affirm "that the common good is better served by allowing to individual Christians the greatest possible liberty of informed moral judgment, and that therefore official moral teaching should as far as possible be commendatory rather than proscriptive and binding."[32] The differing Catholic view is strikingly put in the 1975 Catholic-Lutheran-Reformed dialogue on mixed marriages: "The church has the duty to support and enlighten the conscience of the Catholic partner (and so also his freedom of conscience), since it is directly responsible for his salvation [sie ist unmittelbar für sein Heil verantwortlich]."[33]

Particularly in the area of marriage, this difference becomes sharper when Catholic moral instruction takes the form of canon law. As the 1975 Anglican-Catholic dialogue on marriage noted, the Anglican layperson

---

30. C-Meth Int 1981, ¶46f.

31. JWG 1998, IV, 2, 38.

32. ARCIC 1994, ¶49.

33. C-L-R 1975, ¶81.

finds the concept "law" in this area surprising. "In his ordinary Christian living the Anglican accepts the authority of the Church as a moral obligation; the sense of there being a law to keep seldom occurs to him."[34] The Catholic Church finds the concept "law" appropriate here: "In the Catholic view, on the contrary, the laws of the Church are a function of theology and an expression of pastoral concern. They express in a practical manner the requirements of the doctrine of faith, and are intended to introduce Christian values into the life of the faithful."[35]

Obviously, a significant difference in how one understands the relation of the individual Christian to the teaching authority of the church lies behind this difference in the area of ethics. The more general difference is felt with greater sharpness when it touches morality and conscience.

Dialogues That Deal with Specific Ethical Issues

A variety of specific ethical issues have been addressed in ecumenical dialogues.

Marriage and Divorce

By far, the specific ethical issue addressed by the largest number of dialogues is marriage. Especially in the 1970s, the topic was taken up with the pastoral issue of confessionally mixed marriages in mind, but the larger ethical questions related to marriage were also discussed. As Appendix B shows, these dialogues mostly come from the 1970s and may not fully represent where the churches stand on these matters today.

The dialogues manifest no disagreement on the nature and ends of marriage or its divine institution. Typical here is the conclusion of the 1975 Anglican-Catholic dialogue on marriage and mixed marriage: "On marriage itself the Commission finds no fundamental difference of doctrine between the two Churches, as regards what marriage of its nature is or the ends which it is ordained to serve."[36] While most of the dialogues mention procreation and the raising of children as one aspect of marriage, only one dialogue explicitly affirmed that the deliberate exclusion of children from a marriage violates its nature. In 1994, ARCIC stated as a common assertion:

34. A-C Int 1975, ¶25.
35. C-L-R 1975, ¶96.
36. A-C Int 1975, ¶21.

"A deliberate decision, therefore, without justifiable reason, to exclude pro-creation from a marriage is a rejection of this good and a contradiction of the nature of marriage itself."[37] Disagreement in this dialogue appeared only over the question whether the good of procreation is a norm governing a marriage as a whole or governing each act of intercourse (i.e., whether artificial birth control is permissible for family planning or not permissible at all).[38]

A significant range of non-Catholic, non-Orthodox churches (Anglican, Disciples, Methodist) were open in dialogue to speak of marriage as sacramental, if not a sacrament. Dissent was registered in the Catholic-Lutheran-Reformed dialogue on marriage, in which the Protestant participants stated that marriage does not itself give grace, but receives it.[39] Nevertheless, the dialogue stated that they had come "decisively closer" to a common understanding of marriage[40] and that they had achieved "a view of marriage which is in a profound sense a common one."[41]

All dialogues on marriage affirm its essentially permanent and life-long character. Disagreement arises over whether a marriage can so break down or die as to permit divorce and remarriage and over the significance of difference on this question. Here the Catholic-Orthodox precedent is widely cited. While the Catholic Church does not permit divorce and re-marriage following a sacramental marriage, the Orthodox Church (quoting a statement from the Joint Commission of Catholic and Orthodox Bishops) "following Mt 19:9 . . . permits divorce under certain circumstances, not only in the case of adultery [mentioned in Mt 19:9] but also of other serious assaults on the moral and spiritual foundation of marriage (secret abortion, endangering the life of the spouse, forcing the spouse to prostitution and similar abusive situations)." Persons entering a second marriage, however, "are subject to penance even in the case of widows and widowers."[42] The two US Catholic-Orthodox dialogues that have taken up marriage both conclude that Catholic-Orthodox differences on marriage "pertain more to the level of secondary theological reflection than to that of dogma,"[43]

---

37. ARCIC 1994, ¶78.
38. Ibid., ¶80.
39. C-L-R 1975, ¶12.
40. Ibid., ¶102.
41. Ibid., ¶18.
42. C-O USA 1990, 501.
43. C-O USA 1978, 337; C-O USA 1990, 500.

although the later, 1990 dialogue of bishops uses this phrase explicitly only in relation to the differences over "the required ecclesial context for marriage," that is, over who is the minister of the sacrament and the nature of the requirement for the presence of an ordained minister.

The Catholic-Orthodox precedent is widely cited as an example of differentiated consensus on ethical matters: a basic consensus on the essentially lifelong character of marriage is capable of bearing a difference in practice in the face of marital breakdown. The significance of the precedent is that the Catholic Church, and not just its dialogue representatives, does not appear to see this difference in practice as a decisive obstacle to communion. The international Lutheran-Catholic dialogue notes that the relevant canon of the Council of Trent,[44] while condemning those who say that the Catholic Church "errs" in its teaching and practice on divorce, carefully avoids condemning Orthodox practice on divorce.[45] The Anglican-Catholic dialogue on marriage notes that Paul VI could describe Catholic-Orthodox communion as "almost perfect," despite difference on this point.[46] Both the 1975 Anglican-Catholic dialogue on marriage (§49) and the 1994 ARCIC statement on *Life in Christ* (§77) thus conclude that the Anglican-Catholic difference on divorce need not be church-dividing.

A caveat does need to be noted. Significant for the apparent Catholic perception in these dialogues that a practice of divorce need not be church-dividing were the limitations on remarriage in the Church of England (at least in 1975) and the practice of penance attached to remarriage in the Orthodox Church. In the 1975 dialogue with Anglicans, Catholics explicitly mention changes in practice in the Episcopal Church in the USA, loosening such limitations (Canon 18, Tit. I), "which appear to them to compromise the doctrine of indissolubility."[47] The question arises at what point differences of practice compromise claimed agreement on principles or values.

Finally in relation to marriage, the African Instituted Churches-Reformed dialogue of 1999 is the only dialogue I know of that has taken up the question of polygamy. It reports: "We are agreed that the Christian ideal of marriage is faithful monogamy, but we recognize that some African

44. Session 24, Canons on Marriage, 7; Denzinger, ¶1807.

45. C-L Int 1985, ¶65; Trent also cited in the 1975 C-L-R dialogue on marriage, ¶32.

46. A-C Int 1975, ¶55. See Paul VI's letter to Patriarch Athenagoras, Feb 8, 1971, in *Towards the Healing of Schism: The Sees of Rome and Constantinople: Public Statements and Correspondence between the Holy See and the Ecumenical Patriarchate 1958–1984*, ed. E. J. Stormon (New York: Paulist, 1987) 232.

47. A-C Int 1975, ¶45.

churches need time to work out the theological and pastoral implications of this principle."[48]

Homosexuality

Some dialogues on marriage make passing reference to marriage involving "a man and a woman,"[49] but these remarks do not, in context, appear to have a rejection of homosexual practice or partnership explicitly in mind. I have found only two ecumenical dialogues that have explicitly discussed homosexuality. The US Lutheran-Anglican statement *Implications of the Gospel* discussed varying views on homosexuality without taking any position (§119). The ARCIC statement on *Life in Christ* states that both communions "affirm that a faithful and lifelong marriage between a man and a woman provides the normative context for a fully sexual relationship . . . Both reject, therefore, the claim, sometimes made, that homosexual relationship and married relationship are morally equivalent, and equally capable of expressing the right ordering and use of the sexual drive." After noting Catholic teaching that "homosexual activity is 'intrinsically disordered,'" the dialogue adds: "Anglicans could agree that such activity is disordered; but there may well be differences among them in the consequent moral and pastoral advice they would think it right to offer to those seeking their counsel and direction." The dialogue comments, "Here again our different approaches to the formulation of law are relevant."[50]

While questions related to homosexuality have been vehemently debated within our churches, they have not yet been taken up in detail in ecumenical dialogues. My general experience (particularly from my time in the 1990s as WCC observer to ARCIC while it addressed the ordination of women) is that when a question is controversial within one or more of the involved churches, the present structures of ecumenical dialogue do not advance discussion. We have yet to find a useful forum for an ecumenical discussion of such issues.

48. AIC-R Int 1999, ¶11.

49. C-O USA 1978, 335; OC-O 1987, 262; C- Meth 1971, ¶71.

50. All quotations from ¶87.

War and Peace

Questions of war and peace have been prominent, as one might expect, in dialogues that have included the historic peace churches, especially the Mennonites. Such dialogues have agreed that either Christians[51] or the churches[52] (language in different dialogues varies; whether intentionally is hard to tell) are called to be peacemakers in the world. The language used in this context is quite strong. The Faith and Order Commission of the NCC states: "We consider this [the call to be peacemakers] a common confession of the faith once delivered to the apostles, basic to our Christian unity."[53] The Catholic-Mennonite international dialogue states: "reconciliation, non-violence and active peace-making belong to the heart of the gospel."[54]

The US Lutheran-Mennonite dialogue expressed an "unequivocal rejection" of nuclear war.[55] In 1985, in the shadow of the intensified Cold War of the time, the US Catholic-Reformed dialogue went further and declared: "Preparation for nuclear war is morally intolerable,"[56] apparently condemning nuclear deterrence.

Nevertheless, the gap between the rejection of all participation in warfare by the historic peace churches and the limited acceptance of such participation by other churches remains unbridged in these dialogues. Various churches (Baptist, Catholic, Lutheran) affirm a "limited use of force as a last resort (the just war)."[57] Often in the dialogues, such churches affirm a renewed commitment to peacemaking and the pursuit of the justice that makes for peace,[58] but the traditional affirmation that violence and injustice must sometimes be opposed "even by the use of disciplined opposing force"[59] remains in place.

We again here encounter an asymmetrical evaluation of the ethical difference. In the dialogues, the churches in conversation with the HPCs do not reject pacifism as incompatible with the gospel or an obstacle to

---

51. F & O USA 1995, ¶7; C-R USA 1985, 431.

52. C-Men 2003, ¶175.

53. F & O USA 1995, ¶7.

54. C-Men 2003, ¶179.

55. L-Men USA 2004, ¶26.

56. C-R USA, 432.

57. C-Men Int 2003, ¶157.

58. For example, F & O USA 1991, ¶8; C-Men Int 2003, ¶156; A-R Int 1984, ¶18.

59. C-L Int 1994, ¶267.

communion (although some church confessions do condemn such teaching[60]). The HPCs see the refusal to participate in war as "a fundamental dimension of the gospel."[61] As the Faith and Order Commission of the NCC put it: "For them [the HPCs], differences among the churches on issues of Christian participation in violence and war stand in the way of confessing a common faith."[62] Agreement on certain basic values is undercut by a concrete question of practice: does the Christian participate in war?

Abortion

In the immediate wake of *Roe v. Wade*, the US Catholic-Orthodox dialogue affirmed the "right of the unborn to life" in 1974.[63] A difference over abortion is registered, however, in the 1980 US Catholic-Reformed dialogue. While agreement is noted on respect for human life and the ultimate responsibility of individual conscience, divergence is spelled out on the meaning of personhood, the rights of the unborn in situations of conflict, the role of civil law, and the interrelation of individual and communal factors in decision-making. No claim is made about the balance of agreement and disagreement on the issue.[64]

While the ARCIC statement on *Life in Christ* devotes only a paragraph to abortion, it offers a more structured outlook than the US Catholic-Reformed statement. Anglicans have, it notes, no "agreed teaching" on when "the new human life developing in the womb is to be given the full protection due to a human person." Some Anglicans do find abortion in some cases "morally justifiable" when "a tragic conflict occurs between the rights of the mother and the rights of the fetus." An "agreement on fundamentals" is claimed, based on a common "recognition of the sanctity, and the right to life, of all human persons" and a shared "abhorrence of the growing practice in many countries of abortion on the grounds of mere convenience."[65]

---

60. For example, Augsburg Confession, Art. 16, esp. the German text, in *The Book of Concord: The Confessions of the Evangelical Lutheran Church*, ed. Robert Kolb and Timothy J. Wengert (Minneapolis: Fortress, 2000) 48.

61. B-Men Int 1992, 443.

62. F & O USA 1991, 497f.

63. C-O USA 1974.

64. C-R USA 1980, 419f.

65. All quotations from ¶85.

End-of-Life Questions

End-of-life questions have been discussed by only two dialogues. Interestingly, they are both Catholic-Methodist dialogues, one international and the other American. The international dialogue regretted that they had not had time to deal with such questions in detail, but they had discussed a US Methodist statement, affirmed also by the British Methodist Conference, rejecting voluntary euthanasia but recognizing the appropriateness of care aimed at relieving pain that may have the side effect of shortening life. The Catholics in the dialogue felt that they could "wholeheartedly endorse" the statement.[66]

Despite the source of this international agreement in an American Methodist statement, the US Catholic-Methodist dialogue explicitly devoted to end-of-life issues, "Holy Living—Holy Dying" (1988), could not reach such an agreement on euthanasia, because the Methodist delegation included some who did not agree that suicide and euthanasia were always wrong.[67] Here one directly encounters the problem that arises when one participating church has an official and presumably binding position, while the other leaves more room for individual judgment.

Racism

Dialogues that mention racism roundly condemn it, as one would expect. Some dialogues in the 1980s explicitly mentioned the practice of apartheid as requiring rejection.[68]

The language used in this context does suggest that racism is a potentially church-dividing issue. As the Churches United in Christ statement on racism puts it: "The church cannot be 'truly catholic' unless it is fully open to all people on an equal basis."[69] The Catholic-Reformed international dialogue described apartheid as something "the Christian church must condemn if its evangelical credibility is not to be put in jeopardy."[70]

---

66. C-Meth 1976, ¶45f.
67. C-Meth USA, 531f.
68. C-R USA 1980, 423; A-R Int 1984, ¶22; C-R Int 1990, ¶158.
69. CUIC 2001, 130.
70. C-R Int 1990, ¶158.

Human Rights

The 1980 US Catholic-Reformed dialogue contains a brief discussion of human rights, emphasizing their universal character.[71] The same dialogue in 1985 affirmed the limited character of government, though more on the basis of divine sovereignty than human rights.[72]

Environmental Concerns

Passing reference to environmental concerns can be found in the US Anglican-Lutheran statement *Implications of the Gospel*[73] and in the international Catholic-Lutheran statement on *Church and Justification*.[74] Global warming and the importance of engagement for the environment is mentioned in the international Adventist-Reformed dialogue.[75] The most comprehensive ecumenical statement (not quite a dialogue) is the 2002 "Common Declaration on Environmental Ethics" from Pope John Paul II and Ecumenical Patriarch Bartholomew I.[76]

Some Brief Conclusions

What does this survey show us? The claim that ecumenical dialogues have simply neglected ethical questions seems false, although one can ask how deeply the questions have been explored. Further work needs to be done, but it should not neglect the foundations that have been laid.

Almost all dialogues that have addressed ethical questions affirm an ethical outlook, a set of basic values and commitments that is broadly shared among the churches. Already in 1971, the international Catholic-Methodist dialogue remarked on the "recurring sense of unity concerning the moral values with which Catholics and Methodists assess what is going on in the world today."[77] In light of the contrast between these commitments shared by the churches and the commitments often encountered

71. C-R USA 1980, 422.
72. C-R USA 1985, 426.
73. A-L USA 1988, ¶116.
74. C-L Int 1994, ¶258.
75. Ad-R Int 2003, ¶32–34.
76. C-O Rm-Cnstntnpl 2002.
77. C-Meth 1971, ¶33.

in the world, what is shared should be more important than what divides us, it is said. The same Catholic-Methodist international dialogue said in 1976, in its discussion of marriage, that what the churches together confess is "severely challenged and widely disregarded" by the wider world. What differences remain "are far outweighed by what we hold in common."[78] In their preface to *Life in Christ*, the Anglican and Catholic co-chairs state: "In the face of the world around us, the name of God is profaned whenever those who call themselves Christians show themselves divided in their witness to the objective moral demands which arise from our life in Christ."[79]

Bemoaning differences that threaten to divide us does not, however, dissolve them. As the churches reaction to apartheid shows, sometimes differences over ethical questions are communion-hindering (and rightly so). A crucial question is to understand such division and how to perceive when such division is inescapable.

Let me return to the dialogue that took up this question in greatest detail, the ARCIC statement *Life in Christ*. As I described, it offered a differentiated consensus: agreement on a "common vision and understanding," the "same underlying values," could form a context in which disagreements over "the consequent rules of practice, particular moral judgments and pastoral counsel" can be seen as compatible with life in communion. Now, at the end of this survey, how does this argument look?

I believe it needs to be significantly altered.[80] I noted that *Life in Christ*, in the way it structures its differentiated consensus, seems to privilege the general over the particular—agreement on basic values, a vision of humanity, a common understanding over more specific rules and practices. A year after the publication of *Life in Christ*, the US Anglican-Catholic dialogue noted that the outlook of the ARCIC statement seemed to be contradicted by the 1993 papal encyclical *Veritatis Splendor*. Most immediately, the two texts seemed to disagree on the significance of the judgment that some actions are intrinsically wrong or evil and on the impact of ethical diversity on ecclesial communion. The US dialogue concluded: "Even if basic areas of agreement exist as regards the sacredness of human life, the nature of marriage, and the meaning of human sexuality, our very diverse specifications and practical applications of these general principles cannot be regarded as

78. C-Meth 1976, ¶39.

79. ARCIC 1994, vi.

80. The criticism of ARCIC that follows is dependent on Oliver O'Donovan, "Life in Christ," *The Tablet*, 2 July 1994, 826–28.

non-essential in moral discourse and indeed profoundly affect the extent and quality of communion."[81]

I believe ARCIC's reasoning misjudges the nature of moral commitment and the nature of ecclesial communion. In short: comprehensive moral visions, fundamental convictions, or basic values are embodied in more specific rules, virtues, and practices. Commitments to such more specific rules, virtues, and practices may be as important, both for moral reasoning and for ecclesial communion, as more general commitments. *Ecclesial communion requires not only a common vision of the Christian life, but a common recognition that the rules and practices of the churches adequately embody that vision and sufficient unity in those rules and practices to permit a common pursuit of that life.*[82]

In relation to moral reasoning, to privilege the general over the particular seems to imply that ethical reflection should move from the general to the particular; that is, we should seek to bring our specific commitments into line with our more general moral beliefs. I do not believe that our moral reasoning does or should operate in that way. I am more convinced of the truth of the specific rule "do not commit murder" than I am of the truth of general moral theories or perspectives. If I find that a moral perspective or theory I have considered plausible in fact would permit murder, then I would not adjust my belief that murder is wrong (at least not immediately). My first (though, after extensive reflection, perhaps not my last) response would be to reject the theory; something must be wrong with a moral perspective or theory or value that would permit murder. Sometimes we argue from the general to the specific; but sometimes we argue, rightly, from the specific to the general. Values, perspectives, visions are not necessarily more fundamental than specific rules and practices.[83]

Practices may also bear a value for ecclesial communion equal to or beyond more general commitments. Practices may show the nature of one's more general commitments. Does the way a church handles divorce and

---

81. A-C USA 1995, ¶4.

82. On the ability to do together all that must be done to be one church as the most important criterion of a church-dividing difference, see Michael Root, "Identity and Difference: The Ecumenical Problem," in *Theology and Dialogue: Essays in Conversation with George Lindbeck*, ed. Bruce Marshall (Notre Dame: University of Notre Dame Press, 1990) 165–90.

83. Moral reasoning rightly pursues a method of pursuing reflective equilibrium. See Norman Daniels, "Reflective Equilibrium," in *Stanford Encyclopedia of Philosophy* (2003). Online: http://plato.stanford.edu/entries/reflective-equilibrium/.

remarriage show that the church considers divorce and remarriage a tragic exception to the rule that marriage is lifelong or that the church has come to regard divorce and remarriage as generally acceptable?

In addition, I believe the dialogues show the ways in which specific practices can embody a community's commitments far more than general talk of values or visions. For the HPCs, the decisive question seems to be the practice of participation in warfare. The general moral vision that does or does not permit the practice seems secondary to the primary question: should the Christian ever take up arms? The ARCIC model here does not work.

In the end, ecumenism is not about the relations between concepts or theologies; it is about the relations between churches. Can these churches live as one church? Conceptual or theological issues are not trivial to that question, but they have the goal of actual ecclesial communion as their context. The ecumenical situation is similar in relation to ethics. We are not seeking a communion of moral outlooks or theories. We are seeking a communion between churches that seek to live out and witness to the Lordship of Jesus Christ. In that pursuit, they cannot avoid those questions we call ethical. In a variety of ecumenical dialogues, the churches have sought that unity in ethics they judge to be necessary in that common pursuit. That unity will be complex. It will be a differentiated consensus, but it will be a differentiated consensus with a variety of elements: basic values and specific rules; comprehensive visions and concrete practices. The dialogues have begun this work, but most of the task is still ahead of us, and it is not becoming easier.

APPENDIX 1

Reference list of dialogues that (to some degree) address ethics or ethical issues:

A-C Int 1968 (Anglican-Roman Catholic Preparatory Commission)

"The Malta Report (1968)." In *Growth in Agreement: Reports and Agreed Statements of Ecumenical Conversations on a World Level*, edited by Harding Meyer and Lukas Vischer, 120–25. New York: Paulist, 1984.

A-C Int 1975 (Anglican-Roman Catholic Commission on the Theology of Marriage and Its Application to Mixed Marriages)

"Final Report (1975)." In *Called to Full Unity: Documents on Anglican-Roman Catholic Relations 1966–1983*, edited by Joseph W. Witmer and J. Robert Wright, 99–131. Washington, DC: United States Catholic Conference, 1986.

ARCIC 1991 (Anglican-Roman Catholic International Commission)

Church as Communion. London: Church House, 1991.

ARCIC 1994 (Anglican-Roman Catholic International Commission)

Life in Christ: Morals, Communion and the Church. London: Church House; Catholic Truth Society, 1994.

A-C USA 1977 (Anglican-Roman Catholic Commission in the USA)

"Where We Are: A Challenge for the Future. A Twelve-Year Report (1977)." In *Called to Full Unity: Documents on Anglican-Roman Catholic Relations 1966–1983*, edited by Joseph W. Witmer and J. Robert Wright, 160–74. Washington, DC: United States Catholic Conference, 1986.

Appendix 1

A-C USA 1995 (Anglican-Roman Catholic Commission in the USA)

"Christian Ethics in the Ecumenical Dialogue: Anglican-Roman Catholic International Commission II and Recent Papal Teaching (1995)." In *Growing Consensus II: Church Dialogues in the United States, 1992–2004*, edited by Lydia Veliko and Jeffrey Gros, 297–301. Washington, DC: United States Conference of Catholic Bishops, 2005.

A-L USA 1988 (Lutheran-Episcopal Dialogue, Series III)

Implications of the Gospel, edited by William A. Norgren and William G. Rusch. Minneapolis: Augsburg, 1988.

A-R Int 1984 (Anglican-Reformed International Commission)

God's Reign and Our Unity: The Report of the Anglican-Reformed International Commission 1981–1984. London: SPCK, 1984.

Ad-L Int 2000 (Adventist-Lutheran International Conversation)

Lutherans and Adventists in Conversation: Report and Papers Presented 1994–1998. Edited by B. B. Beach and Sven Oppegaard. Silver Springs, MD: General Conference of Seventh-Day Adventists; Geneva: Lutheran World Federation, 2000.

Ad-R Int 2001 (International Theological Dialogue between the Seventh-Day Adventist Church and the World Alliance of Reformed Churches)

"Report (2001)." In *Growth in Agreement III: International Dialogue Texts and Agreed Statements, 1998–2005*, edited by Jeffrey Gros, Thomas F. Best, and Lorelei F. Fuchs, 296–305. Geneva: WCC Publications, 2007.

AIC-R Int 1999 (Dialogue between the Organization of African Instituted Churches and the World Alliance of Reformed Churches)

"The Kigali Statement (1999)." In *Growth in Agreement III: International Dialogue Texts and Agreed Statements, 1998–2005*, edited by Jeffrey Gros, Thomas F. Best, and Lorelei F. Fuchs, 306–9. Geneva: WCC Publications, 2007.

B-L Int 1990 (Joint Commission of the Baptist World Alliance and the Lutheran World Federation)

Baptists and Lutherans in Conversation: A Message to Our Churches. Geneva: Lutheran World Federation and the Baptist World Alliance, 1990.

B-Men Int 1992 (Baptist World Alliance–Mennonite World Conference)

"Theological Conversations (1992)." In *Growth in Agreement III: International Dialogue Texts and Agreed Statements, 1998–2005*, edited by Jeffrey Gros, Thomas F. Best, and Lorelei F. Fuchs, 426–28. Geneva: WCC Publications, 2007.

C-D USA 1973 (Bilateral Conversations between Catholics and Disciples)

"An Adventure in Understanding (1967–1973)." In *Building Unity: Ecumenical Dialogues with Roman Catholic Participation in the United States*, edited by Joseph A. Burgess and Jeffrey Gros, 58–66. New York: Paulist, 1989.

C-Evan Int 1984 (Evangelical-Roman Catholic Dialogue)

"The Evangelical-Roman Catholic Dialogue on Mission' (1984)." In *Growth in Agreement II: Reports and Agreed Statements of Ecumenical Conversations on a World Level, 1982–1998*, edited by Jeffrey Gros, Harding Meyer, and William G. Rusch, 399–437. Geneva: WCC Publications, 2000.

C-Evan Int 2002 (International Consultation between the Catholic Church and the World Evangelical Alliance)

"Church, Evangelization and the Bonds of Koinonia (2002)." In *Growth in Agreement III: International Dialogue Texts and Agreed Statements, 1998–2005*, edited by Jeffrey Gros, Thomas F. Best, and Lorelei F. Fuchs, 268–94. Geneva: WCC Publications, 2007.

C-L Int 1985 (Roman Catholic/Lutheran Joint Commission)

Facing Unity: Models, Forms and Phases of Catholic-Lutheran Church Fellowship. Geneva: Lutheran World Federation, 1985.

C-L Int 1994 (Lutheran-Roman Catholic Joint Commission)

Church and Justification: The Understanding of the Church in Light of the Doctrine of Justification. Geneva: Lutheran World Federation, 1994.

C-L-R Int 1976 (Lutheran-Reformed-Roman Catholic Conversations)

"The Theology of Marriage and the Problem of Mixed Marriages." In *Growth in Agreement: Reports and Agreed Statements of Ecumenical Conversations on a World Level,* edited by Harding Meyer and Lukas Vischer, 277–306. New York: Paulist, 1984.

C-Men Int 2003 (International Dialogue between the Catholic Church and the Mennonite World Conference)

"Called Together to be Peacemakers (2003)." In *Growth in Agreement III: International Dialogue Texts and Agreed Statements, 1998–2005,* edited by Jeffrey Gros, Thomas F. Best, and Lorelei F. Fuchs, 206–67. Geneva: WCC Publications, 2007.

C-Meth Int 1971 (Joint Commission between the Roman Catholic Church and the World Methodist Council)

"The Denver Report 1971." In *Growth in Agreement: Reports and Agreed Statements of Ecumenical Conversations on a World Level,* edited by Harding Meyer and Lukas Vischer, 308–39. New York: Paulist, 1984.

C-Meth Int 1976 (Joint Commission between the Roman Catholic Church and the World Methodist Council)

"The Dublin Report 1976." In *Growth in Agreement: Reports and Agreed Statements of Ecumenical Conversations on a World Level,* edited by Harding Meyer and Lukas Vischer, 340–66. New York: Paulist, 1984.

C-Meth Int 1981 (Joint Commission between the Roman Catholic Church and the World Methodist Council)

"The Honolulu Report 1981." In *Growth in Agreement: Reports and Agreed Statements of Ecumenical Conversations on a World Level,* edited by Harding Meyer and Lukas Vischer, 367–87. New York: Paulist, 1984.

C-Meth USA 1988 (Roman Catholic-United Methodist Dialogue)

"Holy Living, Holy Dying (1988)." In *Growing Consensus: Church Dialogues in the United States, 1962–1991*, edited by Joseph A. Burgess and Jeffrey Gros, 529–42. New York: Paulist, 1995.

C-O Rm-Cnstnpl 2002 (John Paul II and Bartholomew I)

"Common Declaration on Environmental Ethics (June 10, 2002)." In *Growth in Agreement III: International Dialogue Texts and Agreed Statements, 1998–2005*, edited by Jeffrey Gros, Thomas F. Best, and Lorelei F. Fuchs, 184–86. Geneva: WCC Publications, 2007.

C-O USA 1974 (Orthodox-Roman Catholic Bilateral Consultation in the United States)

"An Agreed Statement on Respect for Life (1974)." In *Building Unity: Ecumenical Dialogues with Roman Catholic Participation in the United States*, edited by Joseph A. Burgess and Jeffrey Gros, 328–29. New York: Paulist, 1989.

C-O USA 1978 (Orthodox-Roman Catholic Bilateral Consultation in the United States)

"An Agreed Statement on the Sanctity of Marriage (1978)." In *Building Unity: Ecumenical Dialogues with Roman Catholic Participation in the United States*, edited by Joseph A. Burgess and Jeffrey Gros, 335–38. New York: Paulist, 1989.

C-O USA 1990 (Joint Committee of Orthodox and Roman Catholic Bishops in the United States)

"A Pastoral Statement on Marriage (1990)." In *Growing Consensus: Church Dialogues in the United States, 1962–1991*, edited by Joseph A. Burgess and Jeffrey Gros, 497–504. New York: Paulist, 1995.

C-R Int 1990 (Reformed-Roman Catholic International Dialogue)

"Towards a Common Understanding of the Church (1990)." In *Growth in Agreement II: Reports and Agreed Statements of Ecumenical Conversations on a World Level, 1982–1998*, edited by Jeffrey Gros, Harding Meyer, and William G. Rusch, 780–818. Geneva: WCC Publications, 2000.

Appendix 1

C-R USA 1980 (Roman Catholic/Presbyterian-Reformed Consultation)

"Ethics and the Search for Christian Unity (1980)." In *Building Unity: Ecumenical Dialogues with Roman Catholic Participation in the United States*, edited by Joseph A. Burgess and Jeffrey Gros, 418–23. New York: Paulist, 1989.

C-R USA 1985 (Roman Catholic/Presbyterian-Reformed Consultation)

"Partners in Peace and Education (1985)." In *Building Unity: Ecumenical Dialogues with Roman Catholic Participation in the United States*, edited by Joseph A. Burgess and Jeffrey Gros, 418–45. New York: Paulist, 1989.

COCU 1988 (Consultation on Church Union)

Churches in Covenant Communion: The Church of Christ Uniting. Princeton: Consultation on Church Union, 1988.

CUIC 2001 (Churches Uniting in Christ)

"Call to Christian Commitment and Action to Combat Racism (2001)." In *Growing Consensus II: Church Dialogues in the United States, 1992–2004*, edited by Lydia Veliko and Jeffrey Gros, 128–32. Washington, DC: United States Conference of Catholic Bishops, 2005.

F & O USA 1979 (Commission on Faith and Order of the National Council of Churches of Christ in the USA)

"A Call to Responsible Ecumenical Debate on Controversial Issues: Abortion and Homosexuality." In *Building Unity: Ecumenical Dialogues with Roman Catholic Participation in the United States*, edited by Joseph A. Burgess and Jeffrey Gros, 453–57. New York: Paulist, 1989.

F & O USA 1991 (Commission on Faith and Order of the National Council of Churches of Christ in the USA)

"The Apostolic Faith and the Church's Peace Witness: A Summary Statement (1991)." In *Growing Consensus II: Church Dialogues in the United States, 1992–2004*, edited by Lydia Veliko and Jeffrey Gros, 496–503. Washington, DC: United States Conference of Catholic Bishops, 2005.

F & O USA 1995 (Commission on Faith and Order of the National Council of Churches of Christ in the US)

"The Fragmentation of the Church and Its Unity in Peacemaking (1995)." In *Growing Consensus II: Church Dialogues in the United States, 1992–2004*, edited by Lydia Veliko and Jeffrey Gros, 504–10. Washington, DC: United States Conference of Catholic Bishops, 2005.

JWG 1982 (Joint Working Group between the Roman Catholic Church and the World Council of Churches)

"Fifth Report (1982)." In *Growth in Agreement II: Reports and Agreed Statements of Ecumenical Conversations on a World Level, 1982–1998*, edited by Jeffrey Gros, Harding Meyer, and William G. Rusch, 821–41. Geneva: WCC Publications, 2000.

JWG 1990 (Joint Working Group between the Roman Catholic Church and the World Council of Churches)

Sixth Report (1990). Geneva: WCC Publications, 1990.

JWG 1998 (Joint Working Group between the Roman Catholic Church and the World Council of Churches)

"The Ecumenical Dialogue on Moral Issues: Potential Sources of Common Witness or of Divisions." In *Joint Working Group between the Roman Catholic Church and the World Council of Churches: Seventh Report, 1998*, 31–42. Geneva: WCC Publications, 1998.

Leuenberg 1982

Konkordie und Kirchengemeinschaft reformatorischer Kirchen im Europa der Gegenwart: Texte der Konferenz von Driebergen/Niederlande (Feb 18–24, 1981). Edited by André Birmelé. Frankfurt am Main: Lembeck, Knecht, 1982.

Leuenberg 1995

The Church of Jesus Christ: The Contribution of the Reformation towards Ecumenical Dialogue on Church Unity. Frankfurt am Main: Lembeck, 1995.

Appendix 1

L-Men USA 2004 (Lutheran-Mennonite Liaison Committee)

"Right Remembering in Anabaptist-Lutheran Relations (2004)." In *Growing Consensus II: Church Dialogues in the United States, 1992–2004*, edited by Lydia Veliko and Jeffrey Gros, 455–68. Washington, DC: United States Conference of Catholic Bishops, 2005.

L-Meth Int 1984 (Lutheran-Methodist Joint Commission)

The Church: Community of Grace. Lake Junaluska, NC: World Methodist Council, 1984.

L-R Int 1989 (Joint Commission of the Lutheran World Federation and the World Alliance of Reformed Churches)

Toward Church Fellowship. Geneva: Lutheran World Federation, 1989.

L-R USA 1966 (USA Lutheran-Reformed Dialogue)

Marburg Revisited: A Reexamination of Lutheran and Reformed Traditions. Edited by Paul C. Empie and James I. McCord. Minneapolis: Augsburg, 1966.

L-R USA 1993 (USA Lutheran-Reformed Committee for Theological Conversations)

A Common Calling: The Witness of Our Reformation Churches in North America Today: The Report of the Lutheran-Reformed Committee for Theological Conversations, 1988–1992. Edited by Keith F. Nickle and Timothy F. Lull. Minneapolis: Augsburg, 1993.

OC-O Int 1987 (Joint Orthodox-Old Catholic Theological Commission)

"Sacramental Teaching." In *Growth in Agreement II: Reports and Agreed Statements of Ecumenical Conversations on a World Level, 1982–1998*, edited by Jeffrey Gros, Harding Meyer, and William G. Rusch, 254–63. Geneva: WCC Publications, 2000.

P-R Int 2000 (International Pentecostal-Reformed Dialogue)

"Word and Spirit, Church and World (2000)." In *Growth in Agreement III: International Dialogue Texts and Agreed Statements, 1998–2005*, edited by Jeffrey Gros, Thomas F. Best, and Lorelei F. Fuchs, 477–97. Geneva: WCC Publications, 2007.

APPENDIX 2

Topics within Ethics Addressed by Dialogues
(Abbreviations Explained in Appendix 1)

I. Dialogues that discuss the place of ethics in church and the church's communion:

ARCIC 1991; ARCIC 1994; A-C USA 1995; B-L Int 1990; C-Evan Int 1984; COCU 1988; CUIC 2001; F & O USA 1979; JWG 1990; JWG 1998; Leuenberg 1995

II. Dialogues that address questions of ethical method (e.g., natural law, two kingdoms, etc.):

ARCIC 1994; A-L USA 1988; Ad-L Int 2000; C-O Rm-Cnstnpl 2002; C-R USA 1985; Leuenberg 1982; L-Meth Int 1984; L-R USA 1966; L-R USA 1993

III. Dialogues that address questions of church authority in ethics:

A-C Int 1975; ARCIC 1994; A-C USA 1977; A-C USA 1995; C-Evan Int 2002; C-L Int 1994; C-L-R Int 1976; F & O USA 1995; JWG 1998

IV. Dialogues that address specific ethical questions (some only in passing):

A. Abortion: ARCIC 1994; C-O USA 1974; C-R USA 1980; F & O USA 1979

B. Contraception: ARCIC 1994

C. End-of-life: C-Meth Int 1976; C-Meth USA 1988

D. The environment: A-L USA 1988; Ad-R Int 2001; C-L Int 1994; C-O Rm-Cnstnpl 2002

E. Homosexuality: ARCIC 1994; A-L USA 1988; F & O USA 1979

F. Marriage and divorce: A-C Int 1975; ARCIC 1994; C-L-R Int 1976; C-Meth Int 1971; C-Meth Int 1976; C-O USA 1978; C-O USA 1990; C-D USA 1973; OC-O Int 1987

G. Political ethics and human rights: A-R Int 1984; C-L Int 1994; C-R USA 1980; Leuenberg 1982; L-R USA 1993; P-R Int 2000

H. Racism: CUIC 2001

I. War and peace: B-Men Int 1992; C-L Int 1994; C-R USA 1985; F & O USA 1991; F & O USA 1995; L-Men USA 2004

Made in the USA
Lexington, KY
23 July 2019